MW01006187

Our Kids

Building Relationships in the Classroom

Martha —
Keep Making a Difference
and Happy Reading!
— CB

Chris Bowen

Outskirts Press, Inc.
Denver, Colorado

Our Kids
Building Relationships in the Classroom
All Rights Reserved.
Copyright © 2008 Chris Bowen
V4.0

Cover Photo © 2008 JupiterImages Corporation. All rights reserved - used with permission.

Outskirts Press, Inc.
http://www.outskirtspress.com

ISBN: 978-1-4327-2453-5

Library of Congress Control Number: 2008931831

Outskirts Press and the "OP" logo are trademarks belonging to Outskirts Press, Inc.

PRINTED IN THE UNITED STATES OF AMERICA

Dear Reader,

This is a memoir. It is my best recollection of events that happened with kids over the years. Certain names and locations have been changed. Some people are composite characters. Dialogue is how I best remember it. Sometimes second-hand. Enjoy.

Prologue

THE OLD BAILEY BUILDING AND LOAN

George Bailey. Jimmy Stewart's wild-eyed dreamer, brimming passions, sights set on conquering the world. He doesn't conquer the world. He never even gets on that train heading out of town. It's the first image that comes to my mind when anybody ever asks me why I teach. I'm sure I'm not alienating too many when I use the reference.

Like I said, he never quite gets out of town. The needs of the people right in his own backyard are too great, and George just can't turn his back on them. When people talk about heroes at the box office, it's George that comes to my mind. No cape. No money. No moves. Flawed. Grounded. Not a lot of pretense to him. Swinging humbly from the hip most the time. And his greatest flaw? He's too decent a guy. We should all be so fortunate to have this kind of flaw.

But, he is a very real hero. A family guy trying to leave his small place on earth just a little better than when he found it. Still, to abandon your dreams, to watch them get on that train without you, is a bitter road I hope I don't ever have to travel. The shot of redemption you might get in return has got to pack a lot for me to take a first step like that.

And it's really not the whole movie that comes to mind. Just one scene. It's right after George's father dies and the Board of Directors, run by old man Potter, is meeting on business concerning the old Bailey Building and Loan. George is on his way out the door and, at long last, out of town. Every Christmas, as I watch him pick up his suitcase, Springsteen's "Born to Run" plays in my head: "It's a death trap, George. It's a suicide rap. You gotta get out while you're young."

As George turns to leave, Potter motions to dissolve the Building and Loan, complaining that any of the rabble in town can get a loan here. It's more than George can bear. He puts down his suitcase.

"Just remember, Mr. Potter, that this rabble you're talking about…they do most of the working and paying and living and dying in this community. Well, is it too much to have them work and pay and live and die in a couple of decent rooms and a bath...? You're talking about something you can't get your fingers on, and it's galling you." George turns to the Board of Directors for one last plea. "This town needs this measly one-horse institution if only to have some place where people can come without crawling to Potter." The board buys what George is saying, but they'll only keep it going if George stays around and runs the place.

Right there. Right there, George must choose between his own passions and dreams and the needs of those less fortunate. You'd be hard pressed to find a self-help book on the shelves these days that would recommend that George abandon his dreams for the sake of others. George Bailey today might be advised to incessantly repeat, "I am getting out of town…I am getting out of town…" But he doesn't.

As far as I'm concerned, when George is selling them on the building and loan, he can just as easily be talking about public education. Public education is the old Bailey Building and Loan. It's a bit beaten and it's got its holes and gaps, but we need public education. Good, well-funded public education. It's always been one of the last hopes for Mr. Potter's rabble. And it's one of the last places the great privatizors haven't fully gutted. But, they're swarming. I can feel it. Underfunded schools in bleak neighborhoods are now set up for failure nationally so the privatizors can dump their vouchers down and start gutting my Bailey Building and Loan. But, I do have today.

Now, I'm no George Bailey. Far from it. But I can't help thinking that I play a part in keeping my Bailey Building and Loan afloat. The so-called rabble march in and we help them become more. We find the small dreams that wisp through our doors and feed them when no one else will. And we make dreamers out of those who did not know they were even allowed to be dreamers. It's a tall order. And most of us aren't getting rich from it. Free market and smaller government are at the door, licking their chops. Vigilance is a must from here on in.

So here, before you, are just a few of my memories, my moments, in public education; my Bailey Building and Loan. I'm a better man for them. And, in the end, much like George Bailey, maybe they do make me the richest man in town.

Moving Mountains

You're never quite sure what you'll be called on to teach. Sure, there's always reading, math, and writing. But then, there's always something hovering between the lines. Sometimes it's tangible. A clear value. Honesty. Sometimes it's just modeling adult behavior. Good adults give you a smile, appropriate attention, and they show up on a regular basis. Sadly, the kids don't always know what that's supposed to look like. Other times, it's nothing tangible at all. You're just there to guide someone's epiphany. You're a catalyst. An idea, or a feeling, has been coming into slow focus for a kid, and you're just there to fine-tune it. Knock the lens up a notch.

Over at our hospital school, it's been more of what hovers between the lines, and not quite as much reading and writing. Rancho Los Amigos. It's one of the top rehab facilities in the country. You don't go there for aches and pains. It's the place to go when your life has been changed permanently. Spinal chord injuries. It can get difficult catching a kid at the beginning of this sort of tragedy and then trying to convince them that books still matter. So, you're constantly searching for what's hovering between the lines, but the kids aren't letting on.

From the outside, the building still has its shine. New, clean brick and freshly paved parking lots. When I first saw the place, I immediately did some ethnic profiling of the facility. Inside, I assumed I would find the upper end of Middle America, gritting their teeth, collecting themselves, and getting on with their lives. Pristine faces getting the best possible treatment. That's not what I got.

Sure, no doubt this was excellent care. But up on the second floor, it was haunting. Loud, angry voices. Menacing, home--grown tattoos, up and down every arm. There's a prison quality here. And with every wheelchair that blows by me, I look away first. Every time I look down first, worried that eye contact might be taken as aggression or disrespect. I had heard that those small teardrop tattoos just below the eyes symbolize that you've killed someone. I noticed four teardrops and stopped counting. I'm told that years ago, most spinal-chord patients were birth defects or car crashes. Now? Now, it's gunshot wounds. And even though I'm the only able-bodied guy there, I am the only guy that shows signs of fear.

I remind myself that this fear I have, this fear that shows in my eyes, is a luxury item. It's a fear that says, "I have things in my life worth losing." The simple fact that I am able to have a feeling and identify it as fear is a luxury item, too. My life hasn't had many hard knocks. Luxuries, all of it. But in that moment, stumbling awkwardly down that hall, it didn't feel that way, and I wished just briefly that I was harder. Maybe a bullet wound to show. But only for a moment. To be afraid all the time, as many of these guys were, is to become the monster so as not to lose your mind, or to die more deaths than the one you're allotted.

I come bearing a bagful of books. And these aren't younger kids. You can still open up a younger kid with a good book. No matter how desperate their lives, younger kids will still let a good book wash over them and make their worlds a bit bigger. There's still enough hope inside a little kid that a good book can attach itself to. But here on the second floor, we're all out of hope. So I know my books are just a prop. It's like holding a drink at a party. You just need something in your hand.

I find the right room. A gentler face than those in the hallway greets me. First thing I notice? No tattooed teardrops. I take it as a good sign. I don't really need to ask. I just know. This guy was peripheral. Wrong place. Wrong time. I don't feel such a need to look away, either. Eye contact seems ok. And maybe I have a shot at this guy with the right book. The conversation is badly stunted, though. Who am I? Why am I here? I get a lot of those pauses that tell me I'm not wanted, and keeping up his grades while he's learning to lead this new life is ridiculous, and I can't possibly begin to understand any of it – not where he's come from, and not where he's going. And that's just from the pauses. So, I stare out the window looking for small talk. It's a damp February afternoon. Gray clouds hanging low, mixed with So. Cal's soot and exhaust. It's a pretty good view from the second floor window, and I digress right into weather.

"Looks like rain again, tonight."

He gives me a polite "hmm."

"You can't even see the mountains today." Something about the mountains has caught his attention.

"Mountains? What mountains?" I point north through the windows.

"Those mountains. Right over there. You can't see them at all today. Completely covered." He cranes his neck from the bed.

"Mountains? There are mountains in the parking lot?" He smirks.

"No. Right through those trees," I say and he laughs.

"You crazy. There are no mountains here." And he's not kidding. He's a Southern California native, and he really has no clue that you can usually see mountains on a good day. No idea. His world is so small that he missed the mountain range sitting in his own backyard.

"Look," I say, "it's going to rain tonight. Tomorrow morning, look right out past those trees, and you'll see mountains." Again he cranes his neck, this time squinting into the gray sky.

"Oh, now you a mountain-mover. You just gonna woop up a mountain out there."

"That's right." I laugh. "I'm the mountain-mover. I'm going to move a mountain just for you. Put it right out there for you to see. Faith of a mustard seed," I add, but he misses that one.

The next morning feels a bit like Christmas for me. Before I've poured that first cup of coffee, I'm standing northward in my driveway, searching the skies for mountains. And there they are. You can't miss them. I actually feel as if I've had something to do with those mountains showing up.

Me and my bagful of books trot through the hospital school's lobby that afternoon, all the while craning my neck northward, making sure my mountains are still right where I left them that morning. Still there, looking as if they've grown during the day. When I walk into the room, he's sitting straight up in bed, pointing out the window.

"There's mountains out there!" he says with his voice jumping octaves along the way. I nod and point too. We don't say anything for a while. It's as if we are keeping a secret, staring over at mountains nobody knows are there. I look over at the bed. My temporary new student has forgotten, just for a moment, why he's there. As I watch, I'm reminded why I'm there. I recall an old sales technique I used to use. See, when you're closing a deal, and you're at that critical moment where they may buy or walk away, don't talk. Talking at that critical moment suggests that you're backpedaling. It's as if you're condoning their buyer's remorse. At that moment, you don't say a word. You simply push the contract and pen in front of them. And you wait. In silence.

So while my student stares out at the new mountains, I quietly, almost unnoticed, pull a book from my bag and place it on the tray table in front of him. And then I don't say a word. The deal hangs in the silence. He picks it up and checks out the cover.

"I think we were reading this in my English class." And the deal is closed. A lot of times these are deals I'm not able to close. I'm the telemarketer that has invaded their rooms. But in this room the deal is closed, and the book is open. And it feels a lot like moving mountains.

A Mom Like Mine

She never mentioned her mother in her essay. Not once. But her mother was all over the pages. Between every line. She never talked about her mother. Not ever. But her mother was in every conversation we ever had. Every time she adamantly told me about things she would definitely do with her life and all the stuff she would definitely not do with her life, you could feel her mother's influence in her conviction. Her mother's shadow would start to hover just over her shoulder. And it wasn't necessary. It was all over her face as well. She had actress eyes that seemed to say a whole lot simply by blinking. Angelic and fierce all at once. In most pictures of angels, the angels always look lazy to me, lacking purpose. No drive. Like they need boot camp. Jordan had that angel face, but fire in her eyes. Always the fire. I was told by her previous teachers that her face was all her mom, too. A little uncanny. But I never would've found that out from Jordan. Like I said, she never spoke of her. Never wrote about her. Never directly, anyway.

It is that way sometimes. We talk or write all around the pain because it has to leak out. But we never let it out directly. There is that fear that if it all just came out at once, the pain would swallow anything else we ever were. We would be known to others as only that person with all that pain.

"There goes that new professor," someone would say. "I hear he's pretty smart." Quickly, your achievement would be brushed over. "Hmmm, that's the one with that big, broad pain." And there you'd be. Known only as that pain. So, we circle it. Let it out in small doses. Just enough for the soul to safely digest.

Her essay was a winner throughout the district. Fifth-grade finalist. It was written during Red Ribbon Week. It's our "Say No to Drugs" program. Just about all schools have one. Tobacco and alcohol are thrown into the mix as well. And every year, at least one child confesses to you that a parent or grandparent smokes, as if you have the authority under a provision of Red Ribbon Week to bust them. Sometimes they cry because you've done such a fantastic job of convincing them of the evils of tobacco that they are certain their known smokers will perish before Red Ribbon Week is up. There's never as much clarity as you would like when it comes to kids. At ten, they're still pawing their way through a grey world with a black-and-white sensibility.

Jordan knew the crippling effects drugs could have on a family. Her mother had drug problems all of Jordan's life. In kindergarten, Jordan's mother came to school to volunteer. She staggered into the room. Eyes unfixed. Speech slurring. Words toppling into one another. Heightened baby babble, really. Alcohol just seemed to fall out of her mouth in puffs of warm breath. Her hair looked slept on. She hadn't been home yet. It was still the night before for Jordan's mother.

She was escorted out of the room and asked to leave. Really, she needed to go home and sober up. She chose not to. Instead, Jordan's mother stood across the school and screamed about the school, the teacher, and the principal. Twice, she slipped off the curb and staggered into the street. Though muffled, the class could hear her taunts and jeers. But Jordan kept it together. This was her normal. So, like the rest of us, when things are normal, we simply go about our day. Letter sounds and numbers. Morning snack and the jungle gym. So it goes.

I looked for her mom in that essay. I really did. I scoured both pages for clues or inferences. I was a Jordan scholar, dissecting her work. No trace of Mom. Without the word-of-mouth accounts, Mom's influence would've been lost forever.

Finally, I just ask her. "Can I ask you something about your essay?" Jordan nods, not knowing what's coming. "You didn't mention your mom in it." Jordan freezes up a little. "Why not?" I ask. Jordan thinks on what I've said.

"I was thinking about it. Then I was thinking that it would sort of be like cheating."

"How?" I ask, confused.

"Well, most other kids don't have a mom like mine. So it be like I had an unfair advantage. And then I might just win because people felt sorry for me. And that's kind of like cheating. I want people to know I can write." And they did.

A few days later, I was sitting in the audience. A proud new teacher. And there she was, my fierce-eyed angel, bunched up between nylons and hair ribbons. Everybody was there. Her grandmother, Uncle Bob. Her younger brother Miles sat and fiddled with the oversized knot of his tie. District personnel, teachers, principals, assistants, and friends. Everybody but her mom, who went undetected by most. But I sat and listened while Jordan's mother hovered quietly between every line.

A Fresh Dreamer

Four bucks. Right around four bucks. That's what it costs me for the pack of awards certificates I use at assemblies here at school. Nice paper. A thick bond. Standard print. A place for the student's name. Space for the date. Places for both teacher's and principal's signatures.

I normally don't think too much about our monthly awards assemblies. I sometimes see them as a nuisance. It takes a chunk out of our sacred, instructional day. One less spelling pattern gets taught. One less problem-solving skill gets examined. After all, we've got testing out there on the horizon. The countdown has started. No margin for error. Scores must go up.

The kids claim they like these assemblies, but they only like walking to them. Then, they spend the next forty-five minutes picking at the loose threads in their carpet squares. In theory, I appreciate the value of these assemblies. Award achievement. Catch a kid being good, and hope it takes. You hope they make it a habit. But secretly, there are times when I wish I had an old carpet square, too. I'd pick it bare.

I'm daydreaming my way through this month's awards assembly. We've got at least three classes to go before mine. One of my kids is so bored, he's now sitting partially on his head, and I can tell that he is seriously considering doing a small, forward roll into the row ahead of him. I tap him on the shoulder and just stare. It's an intense stare, and I really lay into him pretty good, without saying a word.

On the way back to my post, I hear something over the microphone about a little girl who has made remarkable strides learning English, and a father bolts up, rocking his chair some. He looks too proud to speak and gives me a gentle look to move out of his way. He's got a camera that looks like it still smells new, and these very well may be the first pictures taken by this camera. And something tells me that these may also be the first pictures taken by this father on American soil. His fingers flop and stumble around the camera as if they too were brand new to him. And all at once, I remember something. It's a very broad déjà vu. It's as if I am having it for more people than just myself.

You see, millions of us don't sit around and watch moon landings together anymore, so the reminders are fewer these days. But there are still American Dreams out there. And despite how jaded we natives get, there are still fresh dreamers who come to dream them.

I watch the father walk down to where parents snap photos and build scrapbooks. Posture straight. Chest about to burst. Education and immigration. They've become dirty words here. Drop them into a conversation, and things will likely turn awkward or ugly. But for now, I've forgotten all of that. My little guy is back on his head, threatening to forward roll, but I pay him no mind. Everything's a wash behind me. There's just a small shutter-click, a seven-year-old grin to die for, and my own mind's eye. And somewhere, inside of me, in some fresher, untouched place, I'm watching a new American Dreamer quietly, without notice, move the dream along.

A Very Brady Moment

I'm sitting in front of the TV. 1970 something. I'm probably about eight. Maybe nine. We're sitting through our second set of *Brady Bunch* reruns. At this point, I've seen them all dozens of times. I'm not alone on this one. Walk up to anybody about my age and say "Oh! My nose!" a few times and it's a guaranteed chuckle.

My father insists we watch because of the short skirts. Sure, there was some truth in what he said. Of course, he was lying on the couch right behind us. I could've easily said the same about him. I mean, he claimed he was just waiting for the evening news to start. Yeah. Cronkite. I'm buying that one. To call him on it though, would've been creepy and probably would've started some tension between my parents. I didn't need that. So, I would continue to watch after he made those comments, basking in the awkwardness of my puberty.

There was another reason I watched so intently. A much bigger reason. A reason I couldn't really share with my parents. I watched because I was in awe of Mike and Carol's parenting abilities. I had never known an adult who was able to stay so calm, so low-key, while kids were causing problems. Mike Brady never swore. He never screamed or hollered. I never saw an episode where Mike woke up with a hangover. He never grabbed Peter or Greg by the back of the neck. And, as if this weren't amazing enough, Mike and Carol never argued. There was no shouting. And, just as an extra bonus, Carol never gave Mike the finger after he left the room. And I looked for it, too. I would watch when the camera lingered on Carol as Mike left for work or a client dinner. Never the finger. Not even that Italian hand gesture involving the forearm. Sometimes, I would try to drop suggestions, trying desperately to move our family closer to the Brady model.

"How come you never go to client dinners?" I asked my father.

"I'm a cop. My clients are felons. If I ever went to a client dinner, one of my clients would make a shank out of a utensil and stab me."

"Why?" I asked, a bit horrified.

"To make it easier for the other clients to brutally beat me. I'd never make it past the entrée."

I tried working on my mom.

"Don't you think we should get an Alice?" At one point, I was quite sure that Alice was the missing piece. Having an Alice around would take the pressure off of everybody. Freeing my mom up would allow her time to sit and talk to us one on one. She and my father would be kinder to one another. They'd have to be. After all, Alice would be watching. Public behavior was far more important to my parents than the private stuff. Having an Alice around would be like having a constant representative from the public inside our home. No more would anyone have to battle inner demons. Not in our new public lives. We would all smile because we thought we had to. Just like in social settings. My mom never made the connection.

"Oh, boy. An old bat to help with the house. Whatever would I do for fun, then?"

The other angle I could never discuss was simply doing away with my mother. We were three boys after all, and in that scenario we would become "four men, living all together, yet we were all alone." Again, the kink here was that I would've had to take out my mom. Granted, she was no Carol Brady, but she was my mom. And despite all her antics, she had a shred more Brady to her than my father. And besides, there was no guarantee my father would seek out a Carol. Carol just didn't seem to be his type.

So there I sat, every weekday evening, watching Mike and Carol parent the way I wanted to be parented. I didn't need such a heavy hand. So badly, I wished I could've just told my father, "Hey! Can you take your eyes off Carol's inappropriate hemline for just a sec and take some damned notes?!"

Now, it's summer, and I'm a few months away from forty. It's a lazy morning and I'm watching TV Land with my own two daughters. This summer, we are hooked on *The Brady Bunch*. Of course, I'm thinking about all of this again. I laugh a little to myself, but still can't help but think that had I gotten an Alice in the house, my whole life might have been different. As I again retrace my steps and ponder how an Alice could've been a part of our lives, my eight-year-old turns to me and says, "Why can't you be more like Mike Brady?" I choke on my tea. The words just hang there, fat and thick in the air, while nothing comes out of my mouth. How could it be so? My heart is broken. Doesn't she see? Doesn't she realize how much closer I have brought the family tree to the Brady model? Single-handedly, no less. My broken heart mends quickly, in part because I did not come from a Brady home, and mending quickly was always the fastest way to feel no pain. I straighten up to defend myself.

"You know, Grace, I am like Mike Brady." Her eyes roll back in her head.

"No you're not. You're not calm like Mike."

"That's not entirely true. Every time you and I run into problems, I start out like Mike Brady. Calm and rational. Every time. I start out like Mike." I take a sip of tea for effect. "But the real problem here is that you don't show me any Marcia." And now it's my daughter who looks shocked.

"What do you mean?"

"I mean that I start out like Mike Brady, but you never show me any Marcia. Just last episode, Marcia calmly told her father that she deserved her punishment and she understood why her parents were disappointed. You got no Marcia." Grace straightens up because she's ready to go.

"You don't get to see me be like Marcia because you're too busy being mean."

13

"Only after you've been mean. Remember, I start out like Mike Brady."

"Yeah, for like a second." I can feel my temper start to run through me, but I keep my voice low and understanding. It would be bad form to raise my voice while trying to prove how calm and nurturing I can be.

"Okay. Then Grace, let's remember this conversation. Let's remember this conversation and when we're having a tough time, we'll just remember to be more like Marcia and Mike."

"Fine," she says, and we go back to watching Brady reruns. We both watch and steal peeks at one another every time Mike or Marcia acts benevolently. It's a peek that seems to say, "No way are you that person." This is the secret peek-stealing fight we have through the next two episodes.

Sure enough, just a few days later, there's trouble. Grace has maligned her sister. In all fairness, Grace is the oldest and this is her job. I was the oldest, too. I get this stuff. But the situation still warrants some adult intervention. Of course, there's a bigger moment going on here. I have been given the opportunity to be Mike Brady, to parent the way I always wanted to be parented. And my daughter has been given an equal opportunity to be the model child. Surely, I will speak to her in comforting, calm, yet subtly stern tones. And she will understand. She will nod in earnest and not interrupt.

"You know, Grace, I am awfully disappointed in what I saw in the living room." I don't recognize my own voice. It's a whisper of its former self. A hint of Mr. Rogers and a few parts lullaby. Grace doesn't recognize my voice, either. She looks at me for a moment, just a bit stunned. But she shakes it off.

"You always take her side," she says to me in a voice far removed from Marcia Brady.

"Now that's not entirely true." I have hit my stride and have not fallen out of character, but honestly, the sound of my own voice is beginning to annoy me.

"Yes, it is too true. You take her side because she's the baby!" She holds onto the word "baby," giving it a few more syllables and plenty of sarcasm. And Grace has hit a new high in terms of volume and tone. I'm thinking that she feels obligated to make up for my great lack of voice. It's right there when I say it. I just lay it down.

"You know, Grace. You're not really showing me any Marcia whatsoever." I can almost hear the anger pulse through her veins.

"Marcia Brady is a moron!" she screams, then slams the door. I open the door and laugh.

"So is Mike."

And we're right. Of course we're right. We are flawed and charged and trying to be actual people so badly that sometimes we just start to crawl from out of our skins a bit. And the more I think about Mike and Carol, the more they start to resemble Donald Sutherland and Mary Tyler Moore from *Ordinary People*. We are no Brady Bunch, here. No Marcia. No Mike. Just a bunch of folks. Flawed and charged. And beautiful. You can't forget beautiful. And we wouldn't have it any other way.

Brave New World

There are those events, those moments that change everything. Forever. A door can be felt closing behind. And here we stand. Brave new world. Some of these moments, millions share together. September 11th. Kennedy. Others we share, too, just not all at the same time. Proms. Weddings. Births. Deaths. And others still are small, quiet, sometimes untraceable to those outside ourselves. Our souls are stirred. Our minds are changed. The pattern that we used to propel our thoughts has been decoded. Our hearts beat louder. More tribal. Changed forever. Sometimes, when we look back and see all the people we used to be, it leaves an uncertain feeling to understand that, at any moment, we are one special moment away from being someone we do not know yet.

To work with children is to see, to catch, these small untraceable moments. It is to watch a child pause, cocoon, and reemerge as a whole new entity. And you send them back home, back into the stream of the everyday, and no one notices that the child you have returned to them is not quite the child they gave you that very morning. Birthdays and other milestones are really just arbitrary tally marks on the calendar. A way for us to think we have some say in all of this. But these moments I mention – these are the true milestones. Authentic and pure. I caught one of these moments just last year.

Explorers. In first grade, you don't do much on explorers. You learn Columbus. You cut out the *Niña*, the *Pinta*, and the *Santa María*. You mention Columbus as bold and brave. A man who set sail to sights unseen and unknown. Sometimes, you cut out hats. It is Columbus as an early "Round-Worlder."

Second grade is much the same. Round world, discovery, big boats. Sometimes you make 3-D cardboard boats and sail them across a baby pool. Intertwine some science if you can. Either way, it's still history told by the winners. Columbus the fearless, discovering the brave new world for all of Europe to see. And conquer.

Third grade gives you an opportunity to paint a more complex picture. Scrape and peck at some truth. It is here where you begin to cast a few shadows. Good guys and bad guys do not exist as clear, separate beings. Moments are presented, and today's heroes may choose to be less heroic tomorrow. But the scales never tip too far because somewhere today, there is a villain contemplating great acts of decency and high morality. Every one of us, a hero. Every one of us, a villain. All our times, all our moments, bring with them new definitions. Columbus is no different.

I read to them a book about the great Columbus's arrival in the New World. We get the boats. We get the round world. The class nods and smiles. Familiar ground always gives a little comfort. This book, though, is history told by the losers. This is a story told from the point of view of a young Indian boy, watching uneasily the arrival of the white man. In the young boy's voice, there is panic. In that voice there is fear. And, there is good reason. Columbus comes and plants his flag. He touches their gold. He smiles with all the Old World evil he can muster. He takes slaves. He steals land. He forces his will on all. This is not the Columbus of the last two years. And while I continue to tell the tale of the poor Tiano boy, I have all sets of eyes. I have puzzled, angry faces. And everyone, I can tell, is listening. I lower my voice for effect. As if the words I tell are so important, they must be told like secrets, with whispers and hushed tones.

I finish and close up the book. I'm not going to take the leap for them. If they choose to take the bait, so be it. They are, after all, only eight. I start to talk about the Columbus project we'll be doing. No mention of the new information.

"So, there's my Columbus read aloud. I'm sure you've heard it all before. When you get your construction paper..." A hand, connected to an angry face, shoots up. "Yes?" I ask, acting as if I have no idea what's coming.

"Why has no one told us this before?" I look puzzled.

"About Columbus? You've never heard of Columbus? Are you sure?"

"Not like this." We're now beyond raising hands. There's some urgency here that needs tending. More chime in.

"Columbus is evil."

"He's killing people and he's stealing."

"I don't like him anymore." And so it goes for a while. We get a waiting hand again, and we're brought back to our usual discussion format.

"I feel betrayed. Our teacher last year lied to us."

"No. She didn't lie. All the things you were told about Columbus are in this book. His three boats are here. His brave trip. His struggle to survive. It's still all here. No lies."

"But she never told us the other stuff."

"Well, I'm telling you now. I thought you were ready for more." And now, there is a new kind of quiet in my room. It's not the diligent kind of quiet you sometimes get. It feels very unsure.

"What about next year?"

"Hmmm?"

"What about next year? Will there be more next year?" I think about fourth grade and the California missions and the treatment of Indians, and I sigh.

"Yes. Next year there will be more."

"Even when you're older? Will there still be more, then?" I think about my own journey. Sometimes I handle "the more" very well. Sometimes, not well at all.

"Yes," I say. "But remember. Each year, *you* are more. More ready."

We never get to do the Columbus project that day. It's a shame, too. There was a great science lesson about buoyancy and surface tension woven in there. But I guess those concepts will have to wait for another day.

When the bell rings, we line up and head down the hall. The kids amble through the gates to waiting moms and dads and grandparents. It's the same old parking lot. Same old rusty gate. But, for a few of them, it's a brave new world.

My Christmas Moment

I t can really lean on you sometimes. The whole holiday season. It just pulls on your emotions. It tries to get you to cry. Tries to get you to forgive. Tries to bust you open or fill you full of hope. And Christmas. A new day like no other. We are all Mr. Scrooge on Christmas morning. A new hope for others. A new hope for ourselves. And every holiday season seems to come down to a moment. One moment that defines it all. Like an elegant ending to a good short story. There is usually more than one moment. But quite often one rises, floats almost, to the top. I know because I'm pretty sure I've had mine already.

The Kiwanis Club has a breakfast each year for the kids. Each elementary school brings four first graders. Each gets a great breakfast, a visit with Santa, and a nice gift. Picking the kids can be a bit tricky. Although it's not stated explicitly, it's understood that you're looking for kids who might not have much of a Christmas otherwise. You're looking, without asking, to fill a need. You go with your gut. Sadly, we have plenty of kids at our school to choose from. The odds were in my favor.

The other smaller problem is finding kids who can get to the school at 6:30 am so we can drive over together to be there at 7:00 am. Years past, teachers have gone door-to-door, sometimes hurrying kids out of bed to be there on time. When you go to pick up a child, and in their tiny living room are double sets of bunk beds, you know you've chosen wisely.

This was my first year in charge, and when I pull up to the school at 6:30 am, all the kids and their families are waiting anxiously for me. In one car, a boy gets out and I see the rest of the family asleep in the backseat. There was clearly a little determination in getting there. All four kids are beaming. And they are in what looks to be their Sunday best. A pretty bow on one head. Another is wearing a guardian angel pin. A few fingers have rings from bubble gum machines. They've never looked so awake. And looking into their soft, smiling faces could easily be my holiday moment. But, not yet.

As we make our way into the country club restaurant, our kids look almost too afraid to go in. It's not like any place they've been before. When they get in the buffet line, they are hesitant to take food. It takes me a while to convince them that they can have whatever they'd like. One tells me that it's like Willy Wonka's factory. It's not, though. Keep in mind that it's breakfast. After we eat and sing a few Christmas carols, Santa makes his grand entrance. Eyes bulge.

"Look. There he is," I tell one boy.

"He looks just like he does in the pictures," he says. He's six, but he has never seen Santa before. Only in pictures. That doesn't seem right to me at first. But a friend points out that you might not take a kid to see Santa if you already know that Santa can't come through for him. But he can today. I push this boy towards Santa. He's a little apprehensive, but I know he might not get another chance. And he's not missing this one. Now, his joyous face, or how he couldn't take his eyes off his Santa Polaroid the whole ride home, could've been my holiday moment. Some years, it would've floated right up to the top easily. But not this year. Not yet.

After every kid has gotten their gift, most start tearing through the paper. All the boys get a pretty cool G.I. Joe jeep set. The girls all get a fashion doll set. Very nice gifts. The paper is flying. Except for one of my little girls. She's smiling. Looks almost relieved.

"You can open it," I tell her. "It's okay."

"No. I'm saving it." There is a pause. Like an adult, she feels the need to fill it.

"Now I can have one to open on Christmas," she says. It's not something sad for her. Sad for me. But she's probably the happiest kid in the place.

On the car ride home, I hear jeep noises in the back. Doll accessories are already getting lost between the seats. In the rearview mirror is a little girl cradling her gift as if it were a child. I take time to stare at her at the next light. And for the next ten minutes, I keep sneaking peeks at her. Because she's my holiday moment. Merry Christmas.

My New Best Friend

Stand By Me. I can sit through that movie, over and over, just to hear the last lines Richard Dreyfuss types onto his computer screen. "I never had friends again, like I had when I was twelve. Christ, does anyone?" It opens you right up. Every summer holds your hand again. The line is like an outdated brand of perfume. Someone still wears it, and when it hits you in the mall, the rush of falling in love at sixteen just about knocks you down. And, for a moment, you scan the tops of the heads hurrying through the stores.

That's how it is with those last lines from the movie about never getting back that magic you once just assumed was part of friendship. You make friends now, and as good as they are, as good as the inside jokes and gestures may get, something is missing. Something is gone. It's not you. And it's not them. It is your lost ability to form friendships from magic.

But not me. I've rediscovered the art. Actually, the art has rediscovered me. Friendships like that have allowed me back in the inner sanctum. And it didn't spring from magic. It sprung from work.

25

The principal at my school had just gotten back from a seminar on test taking. The sacred test. It is everywhere in education. You almost hate to spend time on such whimsical concepts as values or building bonds and trust. Those are things that are not directly tested, and spending the time to build better citizens might cost you a couple of points in the end.

The test-taking seminar, however, suggested some of this magic. If you have that certain student, that student who does not do well on tests – not for lack of ability, but rather for lack of motivation – then friendship might be the answer. Nothing is on the line for these kids. The test is just an exercise in the art of bubbling. How smooth, how perfect you can get your ovals is more important that the actual choice. The presenters suggested that for the child who fits this description, the best way to combat this lack of motivation is, well, friendship. Make this kid your best friend. The value of education may not mean anything to this child. Intrinsic worth can still be a long way away. But friendship: friendship may be a language a kid like this speaks. A kid, like Jose.

The old art came back quickly. Quicker than I had anticipated. At eight years old, getting on the inside isn't that hard, if you know how to handle it. First, you can be too eager. Eagerness makes people wary, especially eight-year-olds. "Why my friendship? If you're such a good pick for a friend, then where's the line? How come you're all by yourself, trying so hard to impress me? You're almost forty years old, so back off." Some form of cool is still critical. Just an off-hand remark about unidentifiable cafeteria food may make a nice first impression.

A good second impression might be a booger joke. A solid reference to boogers makes you cool at eight. It doesn't make you very datable in high school, which I found out the hard way, but at eight, it'll get you some mileage. A good third impression might be a small hand game, usually "Rock-Paper-Scissors." Initiating "Rock-Paper-Scissors" could really seal the deal. And, just like that, I was in.

Jose was my friend. Before I knew it, we were rolling our eyes at the same class annoyances. And with sweet, simple ease, we had found ourselves in the quiet boundaries of the unspoken, inside joke. Jose and me. Homework was now finished with a respectable level of neatness. Assignments were now completed. Books and papers were taken out without having to be asked twice. Of course they were. After all, who wouldn't do these simple things...for a friend?

In November, our class started reading a book about Squanto. And the more complicated and unjust and unfair Squanto's life became, the more riveted my new friend was to the page. The written word had taken hold. A good book gets up under someone's skin, and their life is changed. And you can't quite go back. Ideas start to swirl inside and your path becomes a conscious one. Question marks, like live wires and fireworks, start to snap and crack, and the hunger for something more is now feeding on you. All that from a one-on-one with a good book. Jose started to take the book home so he could reread each day's chapter.

"What is it about this book that you like so much?" Jose pauses. He seems to be searching for words that he may not quite have yet.

"I don't really like it," he finally says.

"But you're reading this book every chance you get."

"Yeah, but I don't like it. I just need to know about it."

"Why?"

"Because Squanto is like me." For a moment, I figure that I've made the usual California-White-Guy assumption that Jose is Mexican.

"Are you Native American, Jose?" I ask.

"No. I'm Mexican. It's just that Squanto never fits in. Even though, like, he travels all over the whole world? He never fits in. That's sort of like me." And now, my new friend and I are much closer than I had anticipated. I begin to understand that I might not have what it takes to hold onto these friendships anymore. My adult friends never put themselves out there. No one's feeling their edges and no one's holding back tears.

When new Squanto books arrive, I let Jose keep one of the old ones. He keeps it in his backpack at all times. It's a lot like my old copy of *Catcher in the Rye* that fit snuggly into my coat pocket for months.

It was a friendship built effortlessly from magic. But, it was a school year friendship. A friendship forged on the basis of being in the same classroom. As close as it might get, it has an end to it. They're easy to make. At eight they're easy to make, and almost just as easy to let go. A new one is waiting for you in next year's homeroom. Come June, it was a bit harder on me. It was harder making it and harder letting go.

But come September, I've gotten a little of the old magic back. And I spot him. First day, first moments, I spot him. He's fidgety. About to slip right out of his skin. This school business is a bit much for the poor guy, and I can feel it. I decide to break all the rules about making friends. Eagerness, I feel, isn't such a bad trait after all, and besides that, I've got a year of active service back under my belt now. So, when the moment arrives I just leap in.

I'm passing out books and forms and supplies. It's a year's worth of this and that.

"This is hard work," I tell him. "Last year I had this best friend, Jose. Do you know Jose?"

"I remember that guy," he says.

"Yeah, well, Jose moved, so I need a new best friend to help me with this sort of stuff."

"I can be your best friend," he says, jumping straight up out of his seat. He, too, doesn't see eagerness as such a bad thing.

"Okay," I say. We hand out books and forms and supplies. He even stays to pick up after some of the kids. It's a simple thing to do…for a friend. And so the year begins. They're getting shorter. The more of yourself you invest, the faster the school year goes through you. But there's no need to give that much thought just yet. I've got a speed round of "Rock-Paper-Scissors" waiting on me. Does anyone ever have friends like the ones that they had when they were kids? I do.

The Pick Up

I walk the dog a lot. If you've spent any time driving around my town, chances are pretty good that you've seen me and my little dog. Early in the morning. Evenings. Sometimes on a Sunday, while I'm walking around our city hall, I'll see a family or two in the parking lot. Actually, it's partial families. Usually, it's a dad and a kid or two. Sometimes, I notice a dad holding a hamster or rabbit cage. They too are part of the weekend arrangement. I don't know if rabbits and hamsters are legally written into court orders, but I'm guessing if you're a weekend dad, you don't want to upset anyone so you lug pets back and forth.

While I watch, I realize that these kinds of pick-ups are going on all across America. Thousands of dads, waiting at thousands of drop-off sights, holding scores of cages. Right away, I'm wondering why these dads aren't pulling up in driveways? Why not door-to-door service? Then, I realize where I am. I'm in front of the police department. It's right next to our city hall building. This drop-off spot must be in the language of the visitation agreement. I watch children standing very still in front of Dad's car up on the curb. It's almost as if this exact spot is their spot that has been mandated by the courts. And, at this point in the weekend, there doesn't seem to be any talking left to do. Very little eye contact as well. I can't help but think that this is the moment of reflection for most dads. Maybe they're thinking, yet again, about how the courts actually found it best if they returned their children to Mom in front of a police station because adults couldn't be trusted with a more civil arrangement. Usually, when I think of dads who need to pick up and drop off in front of a police station, I tend to profile. Big barreled drunks. Toothless. Always in mid-rage. But none of these guys match my vision. Quiet, unassuming. Middle-management types. Most look like they've never broken anybody's nose or thrown a round-house in a bar fight. Just regular guys, holding hamster wheels in front of the police station at 6 pm sharp on a Sunday evening. Standing around and sighing.

I usually divert my eyes. Eye contact feels too much like gawking; too disrespectful. But the other night, a little voice peeped up from the curb.

"Mr. Bowen! Mr. Bowen!" I look over and there's Gina. Her dad is standing a few feet away, as per the arrangement, and he's holding a Little Mermaid backpack. His smile couldn't be more awkward. His eye contact is brief and he immediately pretends to rummage through the backpack, as if randomly, at this moment, he has decided to double-check for her toothbrush or favorite stuffed animal. I smile and say hello. And I figure that will be it. Social norms tell me to move along. But then, another social norm begins to take precedence here. I am a teacher wearing shorts and a t-shirt out walking a dog on a Sunday. Protocol clearly states that Gina must take advantage of this situation. To see a teacher off school property is a big deal. It requires much fanfare.

"Mr. Bowen, is that your dog?"

"Yep."

"Can I pet him?" The dog is small and friendly. He lies in front of her. Tongue out, belly up. It's a no-brainer. She pets the dog that jumps all over her and now we're into full - on playing with the dog.

Dad and I don't have to make eye contact. We stay fixated on Gina and the dog. I can sense Dad's need to say something. It's his need to explain it all, explain why a reasonable guy like himself is standing there. But I know he won't. He can't. Standing in front of the police station clutching a Little Mermaid backpack has cost him all his credibility. If he blames Mom, he's a schmuck. Really, any explanation comes back to schmuck. It's pointless.

After a few moments, I start to worry about something else. What if Mom shows up right now? I clearly don't want to be part of the pick-up. Dad checks his watch. I suspect he has the same concern. He tries to push a little.

"Okay, Gina. That's enough. Don't bother poor Mr. Bowen." My normal response is usually that it's no problem. But I take advantage of Dad's interference and say my good-byes. I smile and walk on. I don't look back. I don't need to. The image of a nervous father wanting to get rid of me before his ex-wife shows up stays with me for quite a while.

All I can think about is what is being missed. He's missing five story nights, five dinner conversations, five nights of homework help. He misses them all every week. Twenty nights a month. At a minimum, he's missing twenty nights a month. 240 a year. And, over the course of a public school education, K – 12, he misses almost 3,000 evenings. I guess at that point, as the dad, you realize that you're just a distraction. You're something different to do on a Saturday. But you're not home. Not anymore. You're not the part that will last. And when those kids start to outgrow home and parents, you'll be the first thing to go. Saturdays will be too filled and then you're out.

The truth is we don't hold trips to Chuck E. Cheese's sacred. It's the long haul that gets embedded. It's the quantity that allows you the quality. When we try to have quality time because of our lack of time, kids pick up on our desperation. And they know it's not real. Instead, children remember the routines. Every night, my mother sang this little song. Every night, my father would read stories and act out the parts. Every Halloween, my mother made our costumes. Things too small for an adult to hold onto, are just the right size for the heart and memory of a child.

After a few more laps around the neighborhood, the dog and I head home. There are dinner conversations to be had. Bedtime stories to be told. Maybe a little homework to go over before the week begins. Math facts tests will be given in the morning. It's a predictable Sunday night at our house. The girls know it all by heart. I do my part and hold on. We're well into our 3,000 evenings, and I'll need them all in order to stay part of the routine – soaking up my quantity of time, in hopes that I will be kept around as something of quality once my evenings are up.

Learning Language

Recently, I took on a new teaching assignment. I became the Title I teacher for another school in the district. Basically, you test all the kids and give extra help to the ones that need it most. It was my first experience with kindergarten kids. Tiny, shy faces with overgrown knobby knees and untied shoelaces. What struck me about so many of these kids was how little language they had actually acquired up to this point. Almost half of these kids couldn't tell me their last names. Many others couldn't identify colors and shapes. This is one of those reasons I consider myself blessed to be a teacher while my own children are little. It's helped me to fully appreciate the value of helping children acquire language.

We live in an age of poor communicators. Children watch hours of television, play computer games, and generally spend their days as spectators, waiting to be entertained. Eyes glued to some void somewhere with one hand elbow-deep in a bowl of Cheetos or chips.

Sadly, many parents assume that if their child watches Sesame Street or some other educational programming, this will do it. But it doesn't. Kids need to be relentlessly forced to use the language and engage in meaningful conversation. To hear it is only a small component of the bigger puzzle. They have to use it. I've watched plenty of gymnasts on television, but that doesn't mean I'm ready for the pommel horse anytime soon. At my house, we constantly learn the language around a new concept. When an opossum was sitting in our backyard, we went to the encyclopedia and looked up opossums. We talked about marsupials and nocturnal creatures. We talked about the opossum's diet, and all about playing opossum. Really, what we were doing was learning the language of opossums. These are the kinds of things we talk about when we talk about opossums. This sort of thing goes on all day long. Mixing. Measuring. Stirring. Taste-testing. Don't tell your mother I dropped that one on the floor. This is what we talk about when we talk about making dinner.

Doctor. Nurse. Stethoscope. Tongue depressor. Vaccination. Honestly, you'll barely feel it. This is what we talk about when we talk about going to the doctor. The weather. The time. Things we saw on TV. This is what we talk about when something embarrassing happens and we don't know how to handle it. Did you think that was a smart idea? Do you ever see Mommy or Daddy color on the wall? What is the only thing you can color on? This is what we talk about when we talk about experimenting with crayons. All day, and into the night, we just keep getting more language.

The language sets my father taught me were more practical. You work all your life for damn near nothing. I'm counting pennies over here. What are you, a Rockefeller? This is what we talk about when times are tight, and we are tiptoeing from paycheck to paycheck, trying to make ends meet. There are also the silent sets of language, too. Silence. This is what we do when the problems have grown too big or too real right now. Silence. This is what we don't talk about when we fear our questions are too stupid or our words about something may lead to ridicule or cause us to stick out.

When my oldest daughter was about two, she showed me a language set she was teaching her friend Kaylee at preschool. Whenever I picked Grace up, there was Kaylee, stone-faced. I would always try to make conversation with Kaylee. Hello, Kaylee. How are you? That's a beautiful pink dress. Do you like it? Is that a flower or a butterfly on the front? This is what we talk about when we make small talk. Every time, it was the same thing. No response. Age. Name. Thoughts on Elmo. Nothing. While walking to the car one day, I asked Grace about her friend.

"Hey Grace, does your friend Kaylee ever speak?"

"Yes, she talks."

"Really? What does she say?"

"She says, 'Please don't hit me, Grace.'" This is what we talk about when we're getting bullied by the curly-haired girl. This is also what we talk about when we talk about being busted.

I test over a hundred kindergarten kids that first week of school. I force them to talk to me. And sometimes there are big chunks of awkward silence while I wait for a response. In listening to all the kids I test, there is another language set no one seems to be teaching them. The language set of real dreamers. Sadly, many kids are given the language set of scared dreamers. You hear it more in the older kids. Wouldn't it be nice? It's a shame that we just can't. If only. Well, if we were more. This is what we talk about when we are too scared to dream, when dreams seem so distant, so far out of reach, that it's not worth the pain of keeping them in your heart.

So, I start in whenever I can, to teach the language set of real dreamers. I present every possible dream as a foregone conclusion. When you become a doctor, you're going to need these math skills. When I go see you in a movie someday, I'll expect you to read with feeling just like you read that paragraph. When you're my lawyer, you'll need to use those critical thinking skills to keep me on the streets. And on it goes. Every chance I get. Because this is what we talk about when we talk about hope. And hope always starts right now.

Getting Noticed

I had never actually worked with a poet before. I knew a few who claimed to be poets over the years, but they never came across as the real deal. And here I was. So close to such an important contributor to American literature. Right there. Side by side. Working on poems. I had heard Allen Ginsberg read in college. Spalding Gray, too. Went to poetry readings in Greenwich Village years ago. Angry kids, like myself, still battling acne, trying to make some sense of all the stuff we never bother assigning language to. All of them thinking somehow that crooning these things in rustic, smoke-filled voices will give us all a moment's peace. Assemblage of the junk. It never quite does. It only validates how little we each know. Poems sometimes don't give us that catharsis we were hoping for, like what an old blues recording can do for you. Poems can sometimes just make you sadly nod. No catharsis. Just resignation.

And that's what we were doing there together, nodding sadly while we let his poetry wash over us a bit. I lean over and point out something powerful from his latest poem. It's actually stronger than his earlier work. His poems are never titled. He likes to keep things open. Let's them breathe right up off the page. His first groups of poems were simply called "Poems by Javier." All of his first inspired collection was scribbled, fever-pitched, into a small yellow composition book. Paperback. Javier is ten, and I can get these composition books for just a few bucks per dozen from the school district warehouse. And I keep them coming.

Javier wasn't always a notable American poet. Javier wasn't even a notable student. It was my first year of teaching. I took over the class late October. The teacher, I believe, had checked out long before I came on board. Little order. Even less structure. An atmosphere that allowed a struggling student like Javier to simply disappear. When you're looking to go unnoticed, an order-less classroom can be a safe haven. The only rule? Don't. Don't cause trouble. Don't take risks. Don't talk back. Don't show too much emotional attachment to anything, good or bad. Don't smile. When in doubt – just don't. And Javier had become like Carl Sandburg's fog that, "on little cat feet," quietly moves on. When I met him, Javier was down to shadow. Just pure breaths of air. He was easy for me to spot. I, too, had always chosen to go unnoticed. I knew the rules of non-engagement, for most of my own life feeling more like a secret than a person.

Of course, going unnoticed usually means doing little or no work. That's where the unmanaged classroom can help. Javier had been sliding by with minimal effort. Until poetry.

We were going to write a few of our own based on the ones from our reading books. Initially, our only two rules were to write about something you felt and never to laugh at anyone's attempt. If you're going to engage ten-year-olds in the murky world of emotion, it is vital to establish an almost group therapy environment that allows for some real expression for anyone who can muster the courage to put it out there.

Now, writing about your emotions is no easy way to stay unnoticed. At first, there was no poem from Javier. When I ask him about it, he makes no eye contact, eye contact being something the invisible always avoid. In fact, Javier doesn't answer. He stares at his shoes in silence, hoping I will give up.

"Something you feel, Javier. Anything at all." Still nothing.

"Keep it simple," I suggest. I send him back to his seat, and he knows this assignment will not go away. A while later he returns with a poem. It reads

I don't like to write.
By Javier

Now, technically, it did fit the criteria. It was something he felt. And he had kept it simple. But I hand it back to him and lean in close, because Javier was about to be noticed. Guys like us need someone to do this. For whatever reason, it's something we can't quite seem to do for ourselves. I figure all poets were once just people going unnoticed, feeling at home in a sense of shadow and secret. Insulated from others, until someone pushes up against them. See, I think kids sometimes get stuck so far down the hole that they don't want their moment to shine. They struggle against it. A moment that is their own is so foreign, it scares them.

"I'm not buying it," I say under my breath. And Javier gets it. We're no longer talking as teacher and student, but as two guys speaking off the cuff. "I think you're dying to write. In fact, I'm pretty sure you like writing more than you like girls." Instantly, I get my eye contact. He doesn't know what to say. Nobody is supposed to know he likes girls for another year. Maybe two. He opens his mouth to defend himself, but I wave my hand in the air, cutting him off. "Please, Javier. I've been there." I lean even closer. "In fact, sometimes I feel like I'm still there. So, don't pretend." He is shocked that I have cut him off. "Look, Javier, I don't want the first words you really say to me to be a bunch of stuff that's not true." He doesn't drop his eye contact. For effect, I look around the room, as if checking to see if it's clear to speak. "I happen to know that you've got a tornado of feeling whirling around inside. Now go back and give me one of those. Give me something real." I watch him make his way back to his desk. He sits down and, without dropping his gaze, turns his paper over and places the pencil on top of it. Then he folds his arms. Writing is done for the day.

The next day, however, Javier brings me his new poem. Here it is:

I
Don't like
To
Write.
By Javier

I smile at him out of the side of my mouth. I nod a little, too. "I get it," I say. And he's not quite sure what it is that I actually get. True, Javier didn't do what I asked. But he did do something bigger. He showed some defiance. And that was a sure way to get noticed. Whether he realized it or not, Javier was crawling back out of his hole.

The next day, we studied a new poet. His name was Javier. I put Javier's poem on the overhead. Javier is not sure what to make of it. Am I about to embarrass him? I'm sure some teacher has played that game with him before, actually believing that all this kid needed was a little public humiliation. But I'm going the other way.

"I was admiring Javier's poem last night," I start in. "It's extremely stylized. In fact, I couldn't stop thinking about it all day. It just stayed with me for hours." I walk around the room, making sure all eyes were on Javier's poem. "And then, this morning, as I read it again, I realized that it reminded me of another poet." I walk back to the overhead and put next to Javier's poem, a poem by ee cummings, called "seeker of truth." It looked like this –

I   follow no path
Don't like   all paths lead where
To
Write.   Truth is here.
By Javier   by ee cummings

And now, everyone is impressed. Everyone wants their poem on the overhead, next to a well-known published poet. "It's very hard to say a whole lot with just a few short words," I say. "Let's look at Javier's poem first. Now, his poem says that he doesn't like to write. But how does he decide to effectively tell you about how he doesn't like to write?" Hands up all over the room. Javier looks at each and every hand, wondering what in the world they might say. And I can see that he himself doesn't really know the answer. He wants them to tell him what his poem is about. I call on someone.

"He is writing about how he doesn't like to write," she says.

"Exactly," I say and nod. Another hand shoots up with some urgency. "Yes?"

"So, like you don't really know if he really likes to write or not."

"Yes," I say, excited that we're now engaged in a real talk about Javier's poem. And all the while, I can just feel Javier crawling out of his hole, struggling to accept the moment he didn't think he wanted. Before I can process the information and look for a way to keep it going, another hand goes up with equal urgency.

"It's a lot like gymnastics. I mean, like I hate going to practice, but I would never just not go."

"And why not?"

"I don't know. It's just who I am." She thinks some more on this answer. "It's like I sort of have to do it, even though I don't want to…but I have to."

"It's who you are," I say, affirming her statement. She nods. I push a little more to get what I want. "So, how is that like Javier's poem?"

"Javier doesn't really like to write, but like…he can't help it. It's who he is. He's a poet." And there it is. I could have told him myself, but he would've dismissed it as teacher-talk. Now I had real credibility. Another child, a peer, has christened him a poet in a room filled with other peers. And no one laughed. No one scoffed. I turn to Javier and seal the moment.

"It's official, Javier. You're a poet. Like it or not." We begin writing for the day. We never get to ee cummings, but Mr. Cummings has had plenty of moments. Today belongs to Javier.

At the end of the day, Javier walks up to my desk and asks if he can have the overhead from my lesson. I put it in a folder and hand it to him. He then asks for a yellow journal to keep at home. Without hesitating, I hand him an unopened dozen. "You're going to need them," I say. He nods, trying on his new role as a poet. He wears it well. Javier writes dozens of these poems over the next few weeks. So does everyone else until I compare a girl's poem about flowers and unicorns to Shakespeare's sonnets. I use nature as the similarity. I know. It's a bit of a stretch to compare unicorns to Shakespeare, but it gets the job done.

I'm not sure what happened to Javier. A few months later, he was off to middle school. Junior high is no place for new poets. Larger classes. Lots of teachers. It's an easy place to get lost. All you can do is hope that some other seeker of truth takes the time and takes notice.

Collecting Shells

It's not called "Show-and-Tell" anymore. Too rigid. Now it's called "Sharing." Nicer. Softer name, but same idea. There is always a group in the room that loves to share. It is their passion. If there were such things as "National Share Conventions" held in Hyatt's across the country, these are the kids who would go. And these kids will share anything. Anything at all. There is no shame for these kids in sharing a scab on their elbow. Every scab in third grade tells a story. And there are usually two to three interesting scabs per kid. There is no shame in sharing a stone they just found on the playground. Some bit of concrete that every other kid just stepped over to get in the room. A toy from home, a quality big-ticket item, commands a real crowd.

The passion to share has little or nothing to do with the item. Do you really expect to enchant your peers with a broken bit of gravel, or a loose scab? The passion to share has everything to do with sharing yourself. "Look at me!" "Listen to me!" "Watch me just be me!" I don't know of many adult jobs that offer share-time. Share-time at 5 pm. Sign up in personnel.

Very few adults would sign up anyway. And that's too bad. Adults need it most. A few moments a day to remind themselves, and remind others, that "this is me." I am not that cubicle. I am not that office. I am not those budget numbers. This is me. Adults, though, are too busy acquiring, conquering, and above all, assimilating. Many adults are their cubicles. They are their offices. They are those budget numbers.

Of course, not all kids treat share-time as a possible career path. There is that group that never shares. Boys, mostly. They already do not wish to be heard. They do not wish to be seen. They crave the crowds. They crave anonymity. Yearning to fade away. Dodging eye contact. They're already trying to be someone else, trying to shed their skins.

Marcus was one of those boys. Bright, his mind moving, twirling in circles of insight and imagination. The right answer. The best answer. All the time. He was those multiplication tables. He was those spelling tests. He was far removed from the share scene.

Until one morning when Marcus came into the room early, looking to talk to me in private.

"Can I share tomorrow?"

"Absolutely. What've you got?"

"Shells."

"Shells sound great. Are they from here, or are they from some other state or country?"

"No, they're from here."

"Okay, then. Tomorrow. 2:15. You can fascinate us with shells." He nods, then heads out to the playground. The group of shells, usually not an official collection, is a standard share item here in Southern California. And one Ziplock full of shells will inspire many more. I agreed, knowing that I might be backed up with shells for weeks.

The next day, Marcus came early with a large bag. Inside the bag were three lightweight gift boxes. Clearly, this was not your standard shell collection. He opened one and gently pulled back the tissue paper. Eggs. Eggshells, actually. Empty eggshells, still perfectly intact. Only their weight and a small hole at the top of each told you they were empty. They varied in size. Some were considerably larger

44

than typical, grocery store eggs.

"Those are goose eggs," he told me proudly. An eggshell collection. It was definitely the first serious eggshell collection I had ever seen.

"It's a great collection. So, what makes you collect eggshells?"

"Oh, I don't really collect eggshells." He smiles, thinking the idea is funny. "Me and my dad were supposed to color these eggs for Easter last year, but he couldn't make it." I stare for a moment, trying to take it all in. His voice had trailed off. There was more to say, but this was all he was ready to tell.

He saved the eggs. Marcus saved the eggs. His father no longer lives in the home, and he never showed up for Easter. So Marcus saves the eggs in gift boxes with tissue paper. He treats them with great care, because they hold a lot of hope.

At the end of the day, it's time to share. It's all Pokemon cards that day. When it's Marcus's turn, he declines. He knows. He watches the others and he knows that it's too big. The whole thing is just too darn big.

Where do little boys go when something swallows them up? Nowhere. Mostly they just stay swallowed. This one may be too darn big for quite some time.

"Great egg collection," I say as he leaves that afternoon. That's all I can think to say. He smiles back. As I watch him go, I begin to feel swallowed up myself. The fifteen or so little boys I used to be, the eight-year-old, the six-year-old, the twelve-year-old; they too seem to feel swallowed up as well. I go home and think about my own eggshells. Some are still just too darn big for me. I think some more and realize that it's probably time to share.

Keeping The Faith

We start the day with a walk. Just about fifteen minutes or so. Large circles around the blacktop. It started because I was looking for a way to get in P.E. There is no state test for P.E. So, while we may be fooling ourselves into thinking that we are leaving no child behind academically, we are leaving behind a generation of children physically. Obese and diabetic. So we start each day with a walk. And besides, I was looking to drop ten pounds myself.

But more than walking, we were opening up discussions. Sometimes we were sprawled along the outskirts of the asphalt. But if I had a story to tell, we were a big clump, bumping against each other's shoes as we went. A big story like about the time I worked in a pet store and had to clean out the rat tank. They immediately race to identify with my story. Some have had to clean up after their own pets, and it can be just as gross. Others have had rats in the home. In those fifteen minutes, I am able to give them what all kids want most from the adults in their lives. Time and attention. On their terms. To listen to their dreams and laugh at their jokes. And to let them know

47

that they're okay. And it's not really about rat tanks and pets. It's about all the stuff underneath. I was once excited. I was once afraid. I was once you. And you may one day be me, walking along blacktops once again, trying to lose ten pounds and raiding your memories for stories with rats and fights and spooky stuff.

But whether we were sprawled out or clumped together, Brianna was always by my side. She was never quite ready to give me a full story. Usually it was a dense phrase to weed through and pull from it my own snapshots.

"I get home late all the time. My mom has to go shopping everyday now, because the man at the store yells at her when she takes the cart, so she can only carry like maybe two bags." Your mind races to take it all in. No car. Not much support for them outside the home. Probably just getting by. Also, Mom doesn't want to upset people or break the rules, and will go out of her way to do what's honorable. And if a man at the store can scare her into shopping two bags at a time, then she's probably easy to take advantage of. Like I said, dense statements filled to the rim with pieces of her life.

On one of our walks, Brianna told me that her father hurt his back and couldn't work. "My mom says that she won't have any money for Christmas. But that's okay." She's calm, almost at peace with this.

"Why is that okay?" I ask.

"Because of Santa," she says, stating the obvious. "I wrote Santa a letter with everything I want on it." She beams. "And I've been really good." And she's right. If such a system truly existed, Brianna's requests would be met without doubt. Fully. I look into her bright, confident eyes and see nothing but faith. Nothing but great faith that good things happen to good people. I walk alongside her and am reminded of *The Catcher in the Rye*, and how you want to ward off deep disappointment for as long as possible. It will come soon enough. No harm in holding onto eight as long as you can.

Third grade is usually the turning point for Santa. November and December spawn debates over his existence. I'm always looked at as the debate-breaker. And I always give my stock answer. "Santa's real for people who believe." And with that, both sides claim victory, then debate some more about what I said or didn't say. Happier kids usually cling to Santa a few years longer than others. It's not Santa that keeps them happy. It's their happiness, their great faith in their worlds that allow for someone like Santa to hang out a little while longer. Like Brianna. And who was I not to help Santa along? He had served me well. It was the least I could do for such an honorable man.

"What's on your list, Brianna?" I strike gold. She pulls out a folded piece of notebook paper from her pocket.

"It's right here," she says. Barbie, accessories, and the Barbie house. Kids are like that. They have a knack for never asking too far out of their normal means. It's as if they know not to expect Santa to rise them up out of their current lot in life. They're just hoping for a little extra joy. Her list was easy to memorize, and I realized I could get it all, no problem. I get her a stamp and envelope for her letter and offer to mail it for her. She likes this idea, and that's that. A friend of mine went in with me, and after an hour or so at the mall, the sanctity of Santa was preserved for one more year. Even boosted, perhaps.

Christmas vacation came and went. And on January 3rd, our walks started up again. We were all very sprawled out that first day back. No one felt any urgency to ask me what I got for Christmas. Cologne and sweaters don't make for a good story. But there was Brianna right by my side.

"What did you get for Christmas?" I ask. She glows.

"Remember that letter I wrote to Santa?" I nod. "Well, I got everything exactly on that list." She pauses while we walk on. "Thank you," she says after a while. My heart falls. How did she know?

"For what?" I ask.

"Thanks for mailing my letter." I smile.

It is always like this with children. You always get more than you give. Always. Scratch the surface of the worst day with kids, and you'll still find it to be true. What I got from Brianna that morning was a lesson in faith. I started to understand how it really works. We admire great faith, great hope, when we see it. And as much as we need faith, hope, destiny, spiritual ends to flesh and bone journeys…as much as we need them, they need us so much more. In wanting what's best for others, sometimes we are the mustard seeds that move the mountains. One smiling face at a time. Here's hoping you keep the faith this holiday, for yourself and for others.

Long Shots

I t's the first day of summer school, and here they come. Forming lines. Wondering. Searching. The first day of summer school doesn't quite hold the excitement a usual first day of summer holds. Groggy-eyed, their heads keep turning back towards the nearby park. It's summer over at the park. It's summer just about everywhere. Except here. Their tour of duty has been extended, and none of them are happy about it.

Years ago, when I first started working at the district, summer school was really summer camp with an educational slant. Any kids that wanted to attend were allowed to do so. And they did. You kept it loose. You engaged the kids with science experiments, art, maybe a story or two. It was easy for the teachers, and it was easy for the students.

Unfortunately, for students truly in need of remediation in reading or math, they weren't getting any. But all that's changed in recent years. Kids are invited to attend summer school based on need. Gone are the sing-a-longs and projects. It's all about improving reading and math abilities. Small group instruction designed to meet specific needs. It's a worthwhile way to spend some of your summer, helping kids who need it the most. And they need it. They've truly earned the right to be here.

You watch them in line. More boys than girls, usually. And right away, you can tell that school has not been a great place for them to be. I stand on the blacktop and start to gather them up.

While we wait for stragglers, I look at the first boy in line. Life has not been kind to this guy. But his smile tells me he's still hopeful about it all. You have to love that about kids. Life deals them a series of tough breaks, but they still keep their hope. They still have the secret dreams of the long shot buried deep inside.

And Ricky is a long shot. Awkward, droopy ears sticking out of a slightly misshapen head. And a navy-style buzz cut. Now, I don't have much fashion sense, but I'm thinking that if your head is a bit lopsided, a little like an overripe melon, the buzz cut might not be the best look for you. So, right away I sense that Ricky could use a friend. He and I need to do some on-the-spot male bonding.

"Hey, you wanna see a magic trick?" His hopeful smile gets bigger. "Okay," I tell him, and then I look around as if what I've got to say is not just for anybody to hear. "Here's the thing. My doctor tells me it's too dangerous to do this trick, but every now and then I do it anyway." Ricky's eyes grow to double their normal size. He nods. "Okay," I say. I roll my neck a few times and shake out my arms. He can't take his eyes off me.

"Here's the trick. I'm going to take this finger on my left hand and put it on my right hand." I hold my hands up as if I'm ready. Then I stop. I do my best to look as if I'm having some serious doubts about this. This time it's Ricky who leans in.

"It's okay," he says. "Your doctor's not here. He won't know."

"Yeah, but last time, a little bit of bone fell out. It hurt for weeks." Ricky still wants me to do the trick, but I can see he has a trace of compassion for me. He's not just thinking of himself right now. But he's in luck. I shake it off.

"Okay. Get ready." I hold up my fingers again. "One," I say slowly, doing a little deep breathing. "Two." Ricky takes a half step back, fearing bone fragments. "Three!" Quickly, I knock my two fists together. I drop down the finger on my left hand and hold up two fingers on my right.

I know what you're thinking. You're thinking that's the lamest, dumbest magic trick you've ever heard. And it is. It's all in the delivery. The nervousness, the warning from my doctor. It sucks them in pretty deep. And when I do it, they all roll their eyes and love telling me how dumb I can be. But usually it serves its purpose. The ice is broken and we share a laugh.

I look down at Ricky, who still looks shocked. I keep waiting for his moment of recognition. I keep waiting for his laughter. But it doesn't come. Still shocked, he scans the ground around me looking, I think, for bits of bone.

"Whoa" is all he says in a small puff of air. He hurries to the back of the line. Now, I'm thinking he's scared maybe, and that this bad joke has never gone this bad before. Poor Ricky apparently thinks I now have six fingers on my right hand and only four on my left. And it's my job to bring Ricky up to grade level in reading. He returns moments later with a friend. He leans in again.

"Can you show Hector?" Now, my doctor's warning is no longer of any importance to Ricky. Hector? Well, we'll just have to wait and see.

Yep. Ricky's a long shot, all right. But for the next month or so, he's my long shot. And whenever the day comes that he catches a glimpse of his secret dreams, I need to help make sure that this long shot will be ready.

Making Memories

It's one of those standard writing prompts you give kids. Tell me about a favorite memory. Not so far from "tell me about your summer vacation." Or your Spring Break. Or your Winter Break, for that matter. But these are fourth graders and you need a little more. It takes all I've got to steer the room away from stories about Disneyland or Six Flags. Those are good times, for sure, but not favorite memories. Favorite memories are small, sometimes fragile, and very specific. Nothing you can really get from a roller coaster or a free fall. You own it.

One of my own favorite memories is pulling my youngest daughter, Clare, up on a swing. She was two at the time. Two-year-olds you don't always push on a swing. Sometimes you pull. I would stand in front of the toddler swing, pull up, and right before I let go, Clare would cock her head back, close her eyes, and smile. Pure joy. A true, favorite memory. Very specific. Frail almost. Something that could've easily slipped through the inner landscape.

I sometimes wonder how many favorite memories, moments so

precious, never made it. Lost. Run over by grand stories and high adventures. How many are just lying there? Dormant. Waiting on a trigger to pull them back up. Brush them off. Makes me grateful, sometimes. The other day, the bell of the ice-cream truck reminded me of eating snow cones on an August night with my feet cooling in the evening grass. Bubblegum flavoring runs down my arm and onto my bare stomach. And I was thinking about how the days were getting shorter, watching the sun set just over the corner house at the end of the block. And I was grateful to have it. Grateful to have found it again. Grateful to have lived a life that had room enough for small memories. Grateful to have a memory that wasn't so wounded or scarred that nothing more made it to the top. Just grateful. Maybe favorite memories do just that: make you grateful.

I keep pressing on my fourth graders. I shoot down every generic memory they toss up. I want something they own. And I want them to know they own it. Something worthy. Something to just rise up like morning steam off a coffee cup. It's far too soon for these guys to be closed up. If you're not an individual at nine, when will you be? No time for conformity. Not now. Not when we're dealing with internal workings. They need at least that. The ability to be themselves in secret. If nowhere else, then in the quiet secrets that hold us. At least that.

Allen raises his hand. He pauses. Looks around. The pause tells me that we've got something real. "I remember when I was five. Me, my mom, and my dad, we're all holding hands and we all fell backwards onto the bed. The board underneath broke, but nobody cared, because we were laughing too hard." And with that, we have unearthed our first special memory of the morning. The kind of memory that kept Peter Pan flying long after the lost boys grew to become men.

And the seal has been broken. More hands go up around the room. Laurie tells us about a time when it was raining and she and her parents were in the kitchen making cookies. Faster and faster come the hands. It's as if they have all remembered how to do something. Ashley tells us about a trip she took with her mom and dad to the Grand Canyon. Not the whole trip. Anybody can take the standard Grand Canyon trip. She tells us about how her father told them that the air smelled different the closer you got to the canyon.

For several miles, the whole car was quiet, while everyone stuck their heads out the windows, smelling for the place where the earth stops for a while.

I feel we're on a roll, but I stop. There is something so similar, so familiar about these first three memories. I can't figure it at first. My mind scrambles for parallels between our three storytellers. And then it hits me. It's the parents. These are two-parent memories, and all three are now living with only one. Pre-divorce memories.

It makes me wonder. Is this where all the good memories lie? Before the divorce? When life made just a bit more sense? That was family. That was love. Was. And the present? Well, it will do, I guess.

While I wonder some more, the room gets down to the business of writing. It's particularly quiet. Reminiscing. I watch faces looking and searching for special memories, and I can only hope they don't have to go back too far to find one. At least not yet. And may they make them for years to come.

A Little Justice

'73 was not a good year for me. Second grade. I was the smallest boy in all of second grade and was just barely able to peer over the top of the head of the smallest girl in second grade. And I envied her. Life wasn't nearly as rough on the smallest girl. Being the smallest girl was more of a "fun fact." Being the smallest boy was a lot in life. A minority of one. Now, in case you haven't been on the bottom of anything before, I can assure you that life on the bottom is far more lonely than life on the top. Life being so lonely at the top is really some sort of Marxist myth created to keep the huddled masses right plunk in the crowded middle. It's the bottom that's hell. In everything, it's lonely at the bottom. Always.

One fun game kids liked to play with me was to go in search of a first grader or kindergartner that was taller. They'd drag me over to the center of their makeshift circle for the measuring. And when the truth was revealed, a wave of happy laughter would erupt. For some kids, it was so funny that they felt the need to fall to the ground to laugh, or hold onto the side of the jungle gym for support. Other fun things to do with me weren't quite as dramatic. Play catch with my hat. Tip books out of my arms. Take turns picking me up.

And telling was never going to be the answer. Telling would give my parents something more to worry about. They had enough on the plates. Bills. Work. A fragile marriage. The embarrassment was too great and anyway, telling might just give my parents one more concern. What if my concern was **the** concern – the straw on that camel's back that crumbled the family. I didn't want to be that worry. I spent a lot of my childhood as an elderly man. I didn't want to be a burden to anyone.

Once they took my knit hat and hung it in a tree, just out of reach. I spent that winter afternoon throwing rocks at my hat, hoping to jostle it loose. When I got home, I was in trouble for being late, and in bigger trouble for losing my hat. And even at seven, the irony of my father telling me that hats cost money and that money didn't grow on trees wasn't lost on me, as I walked upstairs that night thinking about my hat blowing in the damp night breeze as it dangled from an upper branch.

In February, there was some relief. Mrs. Lundahl started to read to us *Charlie and the Chocolate Factory*. She read it every afternoon, and I had no greater hero than Charlie Bucket. Charlie knew the secret about how life was lonely at the bottom far better than I ever would. The book was giving me something I wasn't able to get from anywhere else. Not from school, not from church, not from family, and not from any other part of the school day aside from those fifteen precious minutes each afternoon when Mrs. Lundahl brought me the world of Charlie Bucket. It was justice. The world of Charlie Bucket was, with each passing chapter, becoming more and more just. More fair. More honorable. Bad things were actually happening to bad people this time, and good things were starting to happen to the good people. For those fifteen minutes, all was right with the world. The Veruca Salts were being told no.

Sometimes, though, these moments of solace would come to an abrupt halt. Mrs. Lundahl would discuss the book with us, and during these discussions there would be the Verucas and Mike TVs of my class denouncing these evil brats! Jack Gooden, the one who'd put my hat in the tree, once talked about how bad gum-chewing Voilet was and how selfish she was and how she didn't really care about others. Had he forgotten? Had it just slipped his mind that two weeks earlier, he'd comically held me at arm's length, while I flailed away at the air, and carefully hung my hat high in the tree? So badly, I wanted to stand and say, "Enough. So many of you are lying! You are the Voilets and the Mikes." But to do that would be to blow their cover. And mine. It would be too much like telling, and I wasn't about to let that happen.

I don't often think much about 1973. '74, middle of that same school year, started with Charlie and got better. So did every other year after that. I grew over the summer. Not much, but enough to lose my place as the shortest boy. I found myself back in the crowded middle after a while.

And I hadn't thought much about Willy Wonka's Chocolate Factory. Until the new Johnny Depp version came out recently. I sat in the dark theater with my two girls and discovered Charlie all over again. There was my hero. And a new script made him that much more heroic. As we walked out of the theater, my seven-year-old turned to me and said, "I like that everybody got what they deserved."

"Me, too," I said and smiled. She paused.

"Even Charlie," she said. She knew. I knew that she understood. And for a moment, I felt the urge to tell her all about 1973 and justice and my hat. But I stopped. I didn't want to be a burden to her. So, I just smiled.

"Yes," I agreed. "Especially Charlie."

Covering Our Tracks

I remember a story a few years back on the evening news. About a five or six-year-old boy who was kissing the little girls in his class. What first struck me about the story was the language. He was the "accused" and his actions were "alleged." I thought those were terms usually reserved for high crimes. Terms used by somebody who's done wrong, but isn't prepared to own up to anything yet. But these were terms used about this little boy. The second thing that struck me about this story was why it was even a news story in the first place.

This particular school district was looking at taking a hard stance against this little kisser. The school board was considering suspending the boy. Make an example out of him. This is, after all, The Age of Sexual Harassment. When I think of The Age of Socrates, or The Age of the Romantics, I can't tell you how my heart swells with pride to be part of The Age of Sexual Harassment. Really, that lens is a bit narrow. It's more The Age of Covering Our Tracks. It's not about not leaving a paper trail. It's all about leaving a big, bull's-eye of a paper trail. Sidestepping litigation. Leaving no gaps. No holes. Ensuring that everybody's tracks are covered, usually more than once. This poor little boy's head was not yet wrought with inhibition, and his heart was still full. The motions of life must have still felt to be a wonderful dream for this little guy. And, as we all grow up to discover, these are circumstances just ripe for tearing someone down.

There's no doubt: While the authorities had the Kissing Bandit on high surveillance, there were other children hitting one another. New bullies were discovering their lot in life. Those crimes were punishable with a strong talking-to, or a few lost moments of recess. But the kisser? Well, he was worthy of dragnets and barricades. Obviously the boy needed to know that you can't just invade personal space like that, but all of this? I don't remember what happened to the kisser, but I do know how it changed school policy.

The first days of school are about rules, mostly. Rules and expectations. Instilling a healthy dose of fear and concern. During that first morning assembly, before the echo of "welcome back" has even faded from the room, the drill about rules blindsides them. You can watch as the glow of their summer tans begins to dull. Playground rules. Lunchroom rules. Homework expectations. Class participation. Emergency forms. Honestly, if you listen closely enough, you can hear their Miranda rights being read. And now, in an effort to even better cover or bury our tracks, we had a new "Welcome Back" Assembly.

This one was just for fourth and fifth graders. It's the school policy on sexual harassment. Of course, when explaining the policy, we do not use the word "sexual," which gives you a clue about how ready they truly are for this one. If you have a policy, but you avoid using its name, then perhaps it's not the appropriate policy for the group. It talks about inappropriate touching. It talks about inappropriate comments. It paints a swell picture. Then comes the heavy moment.

Are there any questions? Well, there may not be any questions, but there's certainly a lot of confusion running around the cafeteria floor. Most of them still can't grasp why they were even brought in. How is any of this information different from the regular rules? Doesn't "Keep your hands and feet to yourself" and "No name calling" sort of cover this stuff? But, finally, we have a question. A fifth-grade boy, still with bangs and a striped, pull-over shirt, hesitantly raises his hand. So many eyes fixate on him. What could he possibly be asking? Maybe he knows what this assembly is all about. And, when called upon, he asks, "Can I still hug my brother?"

You see, apparently, before his brother takes that long, new walk down the kindergarten wing, he hugs him good-bye.

Covering our tracks. We put a lot of energy into covering them up, without a trace. Problem is, the better we get at covering our tracks, the harder it is to find our way back. And before you know it, you're so lost, so confused, you're not even sure if it's okay to hug your own brother.

May The Force Be With You

Forgetting is easy business. Weeks. Months. They just disappear. It's as if they never happened at all. It's why we need holidays. We all can't remember the third Tuesday in July of '86. But most of us have a holiday to hold onto. Maybe that's why there's so much pressure on them. Holidays will all soon become the snapshots for months and months of memories. They're all that's left us.

Sometimes you get lucky. A song or a reunion with an old buddy returns a whole lost era to you. It's a nice feeling to remember a piece of time you once lived, a fragment of a person you once were. It's this way when parents and grandparents pass on. They take with them big parts of the children we once were. Parts we'll never know. Gone. And it makes you aware of how one day, there may be no one around who remembers the small boy you once were. Maybe, not even you. So, it's nice to get pieces back while you can still enjoy them. I found a piece of great value just recently.

A friend of mine was telling me about her four-year-old. The other night he was sitting at the table, long after dinner. Just staring at an action figure he had set on the table. She watched him for a while. His gaze became transfixed. Unblinking as best he could. After a while, he looked away, dejected. He started up again, this time looking as determined as a four-year-old can look. After a while, he leaned in, eyes barreling down at the unflinching action figure. Apparently, his attempt at something was a failure. He shook his head and tried again. Again, whatever he was doing wasn't working out. She finally had to ask.

"Aaron, what are you doing?"

"I'm trying to use the force." And the moment the words left her mouth, a piece of my own life came rushing back to me.

Now, I was a few years older than my brothers, so when the force came out, I was on to other things. Tracking down adulthood. But just a few years earlier, I too was summoning powers. I had tried it all. I had twitched my nose many times – *Bewitched*-style. Twitching and hoping for something to move or float. Or even better, maybe make someone disappear. I even remember trying to walk through walls. My mother caught me once. It's hard to explain to somebody that you're okay. You were just trying to walk through the wall. It's even harder to explain that you're going to keep trying and that you'll need them to leave you alone for a while. I usually made all my attempts alone. Just in case this was too big, too awesome a power for others to see. I didn't need the notoriety, just the ability. At six, I once heard a couple of hippies playing "Mr. Tambourine Man" in the park. In between botched chords and smokes, they were going on about astral projection. I couldn't wait to get home. I was sure I had found the magic, the world's true magic at last. I lay on my bed and tried to travel out of my body to other homes, other neighborhoods to tell other children about amazing stunts I could do. That they too could do as well. I never made it above the covers. In fact, I fell asleep trying. Even then, I held out hope that day that maybe I had projected my soul beyond my body and had simply forgotten all about it. I tried the next night. Again, no result.

The thing is, I was actually disappointed. Every time I twitched my nose, attempted to walk through a wall, or tried to leave my body, I was disappointed. At six, some part of me actually held out hope that it would work. That it could work.

And that got me thinking about my little friend and the force. There is no magical power readily available to move objects. We all come to know this. But, more importantly, at one time, many of us actually believed that anything was possible. Perhaps, that was the force. Perhaps, it still is. So, I urge you to take a moment. Remember. Maybe even believe. And may the force be with you.

In The Company Of Men

It started because he was looking for me. Eventually, I started looking for him. It felt best when we realized that we were looking for each other. I could spot him about three, maybe four houses away as I drove into school each morning. There he'd be, sitting on his front steps, looking for my old white car. We'd share a smile once we could see each other's faces, and then he'd get on his bike and follow me to school. Matthew only lived a few houses down. Kids weren't supposed to be on campus for another half hour, but he always managed to get in and find me. And sometimes he'd beat me to our classroom door. I'm not exactly sure how he did it, but scruffy little boys with unkempt hair are like field mice; they can find a way into anything.

It really didn't matter, though. I wasn't going to rat him out. I knew exactly why he was there. I had something he wanted, and he wasn't going to find it anywhere else within the tight boundaries of his small world. He needed to bond. He needed that small rite of passage he could only get from another guy. Matthew was eight, and with no consistent men in his life, he was still living in the world of women and girls. A boy needs a guy to talk with every now and then to let him into the secret workings of the world of men. It's a quiet world. Guys don't go for fanfare much, so you need someone to get you in.

Luckily, it can be pretty broad. There's no one kind of guy who mans the gate. Almost any guy will do. He just needs to show up most of the time when he says he'll be there. Having a handful of good stories definitely helps. I even have a few scars where I once had stitches. The scars always give a few of my stories more authenticity. When my own father was allowing me entry into the world of men, he had two scars he liked to show me. He would roll up one sleeve and show me a faded gash. "See this here? Once on duty, I had to break up a knife fight." Then, he would show me an old rip across the top of his hand. "Now this one? This is from a nun with a ruler in the third grade. You tell me which looks worse." Then he would pause and lean in a little. "I seen the look in them nuns' eyes. I think they barely feed them to keep 'em mean. Kinda like they do with hunting dogs." This is what I was for Matthew – a regular guy who showed up, showed him some respect, and gave him some stories.

As a young boy with no decent guys, Matthew was angry, and it would not be fair to treat him like all the other kids, kids with a lot fewer reasons to be angry. For example, Matthew had permission to leave the room when he was angry. No questions asked. Of course, we established some boundaries about how far he could go. You have to meet the kids where they need you and no place else. Otherwise, it's like not meeting them at all. This did begin to put an end to classroom outbursts.

The playground was a different story. One of our playground aides drew a tough line for everybody. Standing perfectly quiet in perfectly straight lines was not where Matthew was – at least not yet. I tried to make this clear to our playground aide. "Let's just focus on playing constructively. The line stuff can come later. He needs to feel some serious success out there before we start to call him on the small stuff." Unfortunately, my explanation went unheard. After a few weeks of Matthew feeling singled out in line, he finally couldn't take it anymore. Here he was, on the best behavior of his school life, but all he ever seemed to see were pink tickets and lost recess time. So, when he couldn't take it any longer, he finally had to tell her, "You're such a bitch!" As you can guess, this didn't go over very well. She didn't appreciate Matthew's perspective on the situation. And Matthew lost his sacred playground for quite a while. He would sit in my room quietly, while the class left to play.

After a few days of this, I felt Matthew needed a life lesson. That afternoon, I stopped what I was doing and sat down next to him. "Look, Matthew, you need to understand that there are things we think and things we say." Matthew gave an understanding nod. "See, up here, in your head, you can think anything you want all day long. That's your turf. No one can control what you think. But once you let something out of your mouth, then it belongs to anybody." For a moment, Matthew looks confused. I restate my basic concept, checking for understanding. "There are things we think and things we say." But that wasn't what Matthew was contemplating. I wait for him to speak.

"You think she's a bitch, too, don't you?"

I lean in, because that's what guys do when they let a new member inside, much like explaining how nuns are kept hungry like hunting dogs. We lean in because what we have to say is just between us men. Like I said, we don't all offer the same secret advice. It's different from guy to guy. It's just the sense of getting some guy secrets to help you start building your own code in which to live.

And here we were. This is why Matthew kept so close to me. Now, I have to be careful with this one. I'm not his dad or his uncle. I'm still his teacher. True, the secret world of men may be bigger than this, but I've still got a job to keep. I've got to walk this one carefully. I can't just say that I am in full agreement with him. But he's not looking for some bogus answer about inappropriate language, nor is he looking for a lame cliché about not having something nice to say, then don't say anything at all. I've got to make my point with just enough "wink" in my voice.

So, like I said, I lean in. Matthew looks to be counting on me. "And if I thought that about her, Matthew, you would never know.

Do you know why?" He smiles big.

"Because there are things we think and things we say?"

"Exactly." I smile back.

And in that little moment, Matthew was now less in the world of women and girls. He had moved a little. Matthew was learning how to be in the company of men.

A Small Price

She's crying. It's a real cry. As a teacher and parent, you develop a keen ear for a wide range of cries. This was genuine. No great windup. No wide-open mouth. Some cries are all mouth. Barely a tear to speak of. Just a loud wail. This wasn't one of those. This was deep sorrow. It's not the kind you usually get from a kid. Adults, lost at the crossroads – that's where I've heard this cry before. It's more a sob, really.

And the kids feel it, too. Everybody talks about the ruthless honesty you get with kids. And they're right. But there's an unspoken code amongst kids, too. Certain moments are off-limits. When something feels too real, they back off. And this was real.

Her teacher is walking her to the office. She stops by my door to brief me. She's got an aide in the room, but wants to know if they can get me if there's a problem. Melanie thinks she has leukemia again.

"I don't feel right," she insists through her sobs. Over and over, it's the same. "I don't feel right. I think I have leukemia again." She doesn't. I'll put you at ease now. Melanie's long remission has remained intact. She is a survivor, thriving socially and academically. Big healthy smile and an easy sense of humor that feels more adult than kid. It must come from a bundle of life experiences that force you not to sweat the small stuff.

She's got some great "Make-a-Wish" stories and pictures, too. She's met Halle Barry and others. Her scrapbook makes for some prime show-and-tell. It's a guarantee to be the center of attention. Like I said, the kids aren't giggling or pointing. They've respected the moment. But they start to crane their necks and lean way out over their chairs. It's still news. And Melanie is beyond hiding it. She stands and sobs. As I get the scoop from her teacher, Melanie tells me again. "This is definitely leukemia. I have leukemia again." I'm starting to buy into it. Who else could possibly know what "getting leukemia again" feels like other than her? But apparently that day, what Melanie was feeling was something I'm guessing about half the kids in the country feel these days.

See, as a friend explained it to me, "Once your child is diagnosed with leukemia, they send in the social workers." You're told right from the start that most marriages do not survive the ordeal even if the child does. The burden is too great for many. Some even make it through the treatment, but the marriage dissolves later. Melanie's parents had made it through the treatment. Unfortunately, they were not making it through the survival. Dad was moving out today, and now Melanie says she has leukemia again.

I watch her, standing, only her head and face moving from the sobs. As I watch, I'm struck by something. Melanie has had leukemia before. But she's never had divorce. Leukemia, despite all the pain and sorrow it brings, held the family together. And now, faced with divorce, Melanie is choosing leukemia. Leukemia is better than divorce. Let me say it again. Melanie is choosing leukemia over divorce. One more time. Leukemia is better than divorce. I watch her go.

Half the kids. Maybe more. They have no say in divorce. Good parents console their children. They assure them it's not their fault. But here's Melanie. Standing and sobbing. Melanie seemed to think that she did have a choice. And she wasn't choosing divorce. Sure, leukemia was frightening. Painful. But somehow, to Melanie, it seemed a small price to pay to keep her family.

The Spider And The Fly

It was a good lesson. Exactly the kind of thing you hope for from a room full of ten-year-olds. Unfortunately, it was all about getting the wrong answer. Or, should I say, the wrong answer according to the test prep booklet. And there's no wiggle-room when it comes to the sacred test. You can't lightly shade two answers and attach a note, explaining your reasoning. It started with my favorite type of test prep question. Predicting.

Now, keep in mind, we teach the kids that no prediction is a bad one, as long as it's based on some reasonable information. Something from the text. Something from their own experience or previous knowledge about a topic. Or, maybe, something predictable based on similar types of texts or genres. Again, no prediction is invalid when it comes from some sound reasoning. So, when they put predicting into a multiple choice format with similar choices, they're no longer testing a child's ability to predict. To this day, nobody in Sacramento has any idea if our kids can predict reasonably well or not. The format won't allow it.

This particular predicting question came after the kids read a story called "The Spider and the Fly." It's basically the mouse and the lion story with bugs. The booklet wants the kids to predict what the spider will do the next time he catches a fly in his web. Again, the test doesn't really want reasoning, and so they don't really want their predictions, either. What they want the kids to predict is what background knowledge some middle-aged guy might bring to the story and what his prediction might be.

The alleged correct answer is that the spider will let the fly go, because flies can be very helpful to falling spiders. A girl raises her hand and tells me that this would be impossible. Already, on tone alone, it's the best answer of the day.

"Why would it be impossible?" I ask.

"Because the spider will starve that way. I don't know what good all his new fly friends will be if he dies from starvation."

She's right, of course. Articulated it well, too. It's a good prediction, based on what she knows about spiders. It's an even better prediction because she chose to disagree with the logic of the lesson. When kids disagree with you and have good reason to do so, your job is done. And done well.

And the flood gates have opened. Someone decides to back the alleged correct answer because the spider can be more selective. He can catch enough other bugs so he doesn't have to eat flies. Another student explains how that would almost be like racism, giving flies better treatment just because they're flies.

Still another boy explains that spiders don't need flies to rescue them when they fall. See, when his grandmother throws her slipper at spiders in the corner of the room, they fall hard and are usually okay when they land. The conversation has taken hold. But our friends in Sacramento will never know about our great debate. They'll only know that many of the kids got that one wrong.

Now, if you're the predicting sort, you might be waiting for me to use the spider and the fly in some metaphorical sense, perhaps making the testing folks the spiders and all the kids flies. It's a reasonable prediction. After all, I did title this piece "The Spider and the Fly." But, sad to say, the state would consider you a below basic predictor because I'm not going there today. It's okay, though. The state can keep their alleged right answer. I'll choose a debate with the latest wave of critical thinkers every time.

Easy To Spot

You can spot them. Boys, mostly. As a third-grade teacher, you develop a keen eye that can sweep through a crowd of small heads and pick them out. They are the boys with bright, beaming faces. Bold, full-mouthed smiles that roll right into dimples, about as deep as they get. They are happy to be alive. Nothing has lost its shine just yet.

They are the boys that relish recess so much, they can actually taste its freedom in the back of their throats. They are the boys that come back from recess with a dark, complete footprint across their chests, and when you ask them how it got there, they tell you that they don't know. And they're not lying. It was the joy of recess, of jungle gyms and kickball. This joy was so intense, they were actually oblivious to someone firmly walking across their chests. Yes. These are the boys. Mostly.

These are also the boys who are quick to anger, quick to flare. And they hold it. Emotions can just run right through most eight-year-olds. Short-burning. They have the emotion, they own it, and their internal workings are still so clean that the emotions get flushed right out. But not so for these boys.

These are the boys that you know in your gut were well on their way to becoming happy, typical kids, because most of the time they still show that to you. But this angry side. This angry side was not a part of their original mix. It's there because the adults in their lives have failed. They have fallen far too short. And now there is anger, and with these boys, fewer and fewer emotions just flush themselves out. They stick. And linger. And they begin to build up.

This is Teddy. Easy to spot. Teddy is the boy who tried to impress me with the information that he had mastered making loud gas noises using his armpit. I told him that I wasn't sure which was more disgusting: his armpit after 2 pm, or his hand after 2 pm. I wasn't sure if it was worse for his hand or for his armpit. But I could see in his face that he viewed this as a true accomplishment, and just maybe I was the one adult who was going to honor his gift. So I did. And it's true, too. It is a skill. I never fully developed it myself. To this day, I'm not sure if it was because I couldn't maneuver my armpit to be deep enough, or was it that I couldn't create enough suction with my palm? My own father once told me that I had shallow pits and little palms, and that I should just concentrate on making my gas the old-fashioned way. "It's more respected that way," he said, trying to console me.

I put aside my feelings of jealousy and let Teddy give our class a full demonstration. And he wasn't just bragging. The sound was strong, loud, and clear. If I closed my eyes, I couldn't be certain if it was genuine or not. And when the class was done laughing, we all clapped.

Teddy is also the boy who listened to my explanation of slavery, when it came up in our book. He listened to how it was not just horrifying for the lack of freedom, for the horrible living arrangements, or for the long, backbreaking hours of hard labor in hot fields. For Teddy, what was most horrifying was that families were sold off and separated. Children were taken from parents like livestock. Children screamed as they were loaded in wagons. Teddy was the boy who raised his hand and, with the nonchalant air of one of life's veterans, told me, "That's what foster care is like."

Yes, you can spot them. That's really taking too much credit. Just keep an eye out. They will reveal themselves.

The office called our classroom and asked that Teddy be sent down. It was to be done quickly. A social worker was there to pick him up before his foster family came to get him. There had been abuse reported by one of the older kids in the home.

So, I hurry Teddy out the door. At that one moment, I know more about his life than he does, and I hope it doesn't register on my face. I watch him walk down the hall. He turns back and smiles. "See you tomorrow," he says, but I know I'll never see Teddy again.

He was well on his way to becoming another happy boy. He was born happy and clean. But the adults let him down. They failed him. Teddy was low maintenance, too. He didn't need much. But now?

I thought about Teddy all that night. Teddy was eating dinner with strangers. He was sleeping in somebody else's room, using somebody else's bathroom. And all the while, he was using somebody else's shadows to hide in. And I wonder for how long will he keep that clean, deep dimple and bold smile? I don't know where he's going, but from the memory of his sweet face, on the day he was born, he was moving in some other, better direction. That much was easy to spot.

Music Of Our Own

As a child, music never started with notes. A good tune started with that crackling hiss the needle made when my mother laid it down on the vinyl's edge. That crackle was the real opening riff. It was the dimming of the house lights. One more fire-dry-pop and BAM! "Jeremiah was a bullfrog. He was a good friend of mine. I never understood a single word he said, but I helped him drink his wine. Joy to the world."

Talking frogs and friendships. Part children's song. The heart of fairy tale. Of course, it was a drunken frog who was buying the next round. Now that part was pure hippie, hoping for a higher and happier world. And that's the mix you got with me and my mother, dancing, full-spirit, in the dented circle the living room furniture made. The music made moments. Moments that my body could feel. At five, I didn't need drugs. I didn't need liner notes or concert T-shirts. I just needed the energy. Pure energy.

But by nine, I needed more. It wasn't enough to identify spiritually with someone else's written song. I craved to make music of my own. Luckily, this was back in the day when schools still offered the salvation of music to young hearts looking to keep their softer spots. Trumpets. They were the hot commodity. Everyone liked its sound and its look. It was considered a socially acceptable instrument. Anyone from any rung of the pecking order could pick up a trumpet without too much prodding or poking from lesser minds. But trumpets were scarce. Demand too high. Supply too low. And the school charged notably more for trumpet lessons, simply because they could. Class warfare at its cruelest. What was left? What scraps were there to offer a peasant like myself?

The violin. Squeaky warbly notes and the warm smell of rosin. It wasn't what I wanted, but the school had plenty in stock. Lessons weren't quite as expensive. I took it. I just wanted in. Making music of your own came with a secret language. Something unspoken, but simply understood. Each note was part prayer and part First Amendment, giving the freest of speech a deafening tone and edge. A sense of self-propulsion.

Trumpets and horns had that big-business feel. Trumpets were the movers and shakers. Gaudy and flashy. Older kids wore their trumpets like car salesmen wore pinky rings. They took what they wanted. The best practice places in school, and the best times. They were a top priority and they knew it.

Violins had that non-profit feel. The strings were public television and lesser-known charities, looking to divvy up the scraps, humbly taking what they could find. An old boiler room with a rusty, inactive boiler served as our practice space. During quiet moments we could hear the trumpets blaring away in a room upstairs, complete with windows and hardwood floors.

But the strings had Miss Hornicheck. A big bun of hair and long skirts like flowered bed sheets. Sometimes, when we would look up from deep musical concentration, she would be standing there, stone-faced, with her glasses upside down on her face. And she had the best spin yet on the inactive boiler room, insisting that she had chosen it because no one would ever go down there, so we could chew gum and there wasn't anything anybody could do about it. She offered Juicy Fruit and Bubble Yum. And sometimes, she'd bring donuts. She would always inspect our upper lips for evidence of powdered sugar. We were a bit like a secret society.

Down there. Only down there, in that rusty boiler room, chewing our gum and chomping our donuts with open, smacking mouths…only down there, two hours a week, were we a secret society. Upstairs and outside, in the daylight, we were not that secret society. We were tiny, frail individuals, carrying around those violin cases like scarlet letters. Whereas the trumpet enjoyed social acceptance, the violin did not. The curvy case begged to be ridiculed. My new, fragile concepts of manhood were badgered every day I carried it back and forth from home. The violin was for sissies.

And then, I needed out. Just as badly as I had wanted in, now I wanted out. The walk to school started getting longer and longer, and the nasty comments were getting louder and louder. My parents, though, were not so agreeable. Quitting so quickly, something I had whined and pestered over, was not in their plan. I was going to play, and I was going to practice. But I didn't. I tuned out for months, never making any progress, and never practicing for more than minutes at a time. Slowly, I worked my war of attrition upon them. Really, I never let myself enjoy it. I avoided it at all costs, keeping that hollowed out, waxy piece of wood at bay.

My parents didn't quite know about the true secret language that music held for those who stayed with it. As two blue-collar skeptics, they revisited my violin. It didn't come down to achievement. It didn't come down to discipline. It came down to money. I have gone broke many times, trying to prove them wrong. And so, that was it. Economically, the violin wasn't giving them any worthwhile returns. It was a battle that came with a price tag. I was out. Free from ridicule. Free from the curvy case.

Of course, it was hard to make eye contact with Miss Hornicheck when I would see her saunter down the hall. You could hear her jingly jewelry coming around the corner. This made her easy to avoid. She would always rub my shoulder and say "hi," but I could feel how I was no longer a part of her secret society. Slowly, she stopped rubbing my shoulder and just gave me a nod. It was when the nodding started that I knew I was truly out. I wanted out, and I got out. But what I hadn't counted on was that there was nowhere I was in. It wasn't as if those who ridiculed me now embraced me, so happy to see that I had gotten out from under that darn violin. I was simply ridiculed less. Nowhere to be in. Twenty-five years later, and still nowhere to be in.

Now, I hadn't thought about Miss Hornicheck or her donuts and boiler room for years. But my four-year-old daughter decided that she wanted to play the violin. At first, my wife and I dismissed it as just something kids say. No one runs out and buys their child a space shuttle the first time they want to be an astronaut. But she wasn't letting this violin thing go. She wanted to play. She too wanted in. She wanted the secret language that knew no countries, no allegiances. And there was Miss Hornicheck's face, complete with her upside-down glasses riding high on her nose. Every time my daughter talked about the violin she was sure she was getting, there was Miss Hornicheck. It was odd to realize that Miss Hornicheck was younger then than I am now. She was a memory attached to nothing tangible. To think her up again was like taking her out of the wrapper. Untouched. Unscathed. Straight from the rusty boiler room of twenty-five years ago. There she was, winking and smiling at me, speaking to me in a secret language that I did not know. It is hard to have a good understanding about knowing what you do not know.

So, violin lessons began. And, like most children, my daughter did not want to practice. But she is far too young to know all about what she might not know if I don't make her practice and stay with it. She has started her own war of attrition against me. Little does she know that I am an old-school-attritioner from way back. She also doesn't fully appreciate that Dad finds most people terribly annoying and therefore has a high tolerance for tactics designed to annoy. So, we squabble. I bribe from time to time. But make no mistake – music lessons are like vegetables and manners; they are non-negotiable. But my daughter is good and stubborn. She keeps trying to chip away at me and her pint-sized violin. But we ain't budging.

"Why?" she whines. "Why do I have to practice?" She stomps one foot for effect.

"Because your teacher thinks it's important," I say, staying as calm and low-key as I can.

"Then, I don't want to go to violin anymore."

"Sorry. You have to go."

"But why? Alicia doesn't take violin. Emma doesn't take violin. Why do I have to go?"

"Because you asked."

"Okay, now I don't want to go."

"It's too late. You're already in."

"I don't want to anymore, so why do I have to?" she asks, her voice getting higher in pitch and grainier against my ears with every word.

"Because."

"That's not an answer. You always say that's not an answer." The whining is wearing me down just a bit. I begin to feel weak. For a moment I consider stopping violin and starting again next year. But instead, a different answer comes bubbling up out of me.

"Because, Jeremiah was a bullfrog. He was a good friend of mine. I never understood a single word he said, but I helped him drink his wine. Joy to the world." This brings her to a full stop. Her eyes bat back and forth, trying to decode all I've said.

"Why couldn't you understand what he was saying?" she asks, not quite sure where to begin.

"Because he was speaking a secret language that I didn't know."

"What secret language?"

"The one Miss Cynthia is teaching you."

"Miss Cynthia doesn't teach me a secret language. She just teaches me the violin, that's all."

"Oh, it's coming. Trust me. The secret language is coming, and you'll know it. And do you know what happens then? Do you know what happens when you learn the secret language?" She shakes her head. "Joy to the world," I tell her. "Joy to the world." We put on our coats and get in the car to drive over to violin lessons. After we're out of the driveway, my daughter has gotten her footing again.

"Maybe you couldn't understand the frog because he was a frog and he said frog stuff." I laugh. I turn up the radio. The two of us sing along to The Clash. There's not much better than hearing a four-year-old sing, "This indecision's bugging me. If you don't want me, set me free." We enjoy music together. It's part of our bond. But, as we drive over to see Miss Cynthia, I know that this is where much of it ends for me. For my daughter, it has all just started. Her joy will be greater and her world will be bigger, and when the drunken frog starts to speak, she'll know exactly what he's talking about.

World's Best Teacher

Jorge was a kind boy. I'm sure he still is. Somewhere out there. I just don't have the pleasure of his kindness in my classroom anymore. And I'm just not programmed to see him as anything but that kind eight-year-old. Big cheeks. Deep dimples. It's been a few years, but from time to time, I still drink from the coffee cup he gave me. Written on the side of the cup is "World's Best Teacher," complete with my picture he got from our class photo. I don't drink from it because I think I'm the world's best teacher. It wouldn't be fair to accept the title without seeing all the world had to offer. I drink from it because it was given to me by such a good person. Someone of such high character saw some of their shine in me. And it makes me proud. Jorge was only eight at the time. His mind wasn't yet clouded with ulterior motives. His word actually meant something when he gave it to me. Also, the cup always makes me think of that fall when I got to know him a little bit better.

It was Halloween. It was also the last year of the Halloween parade at school. The one-hour thrill of walking around the asphalt in your costume apparently was cutting into instructional time and causing test scores to drop. It's not like we let the kids take the tests in their Tinker Bell costumes. A school Halloween parade is even more critical here in Southern California. We don't have the steady stream of chimney smoke or the crunch of autumn leaves. We need to be reminded that fall is here, or we might miss it altogether.

As the kids took their places along the halls, waiting to make their grand entrances onto the playground, they didn't realize that a small era was coming to an end. Their parents and grandparents before them had dressed as pirates and hobos and paraded around the school yards. In 1976, I dressed as Uncle Sam to coincide with our Halloween parade's bicentennial theme. I remember Mrs. Johnson walking around the room, trying to guess who we were behind our costumes. And I remember being genuinely surprised that she knew it was me playing the part of Uncle Sam. After all, I had not just a gray beard, but also two gray eyebrows that helped conceal my identity.

Jorge, I noticed, was not dressed in costume. I didn't get a chance to ask him about it right away. He quietly took a seat on the benches with other children who did not bring a costume either. They watched the parade and pointed out their friends. In a little under an hour, the whole thing was over. All the Harry Potters and Disney's finest changed back into students and got back to the business of learning.

I finally get a chance to talk with Jorge.

"So, how does your family go about celebrating Halloween? Do you go trick-or-treating through the neighborhood? Or is there a church harvest festival you go to?" He seems a little apprehensive about answering, as if I've touched on an uncomfortable subject.

"Well....usually we go trick-or-treating in our neighborhood. But not this year."

"Oh, so what are you doing this year?"

"We're not doing anything this year."

"Why not?" I ask.

"My mom doesn't feel it's right, this year."

And now, I'm not really following. I'm wondering if they've

changed religions, or had a bad Halloween experience in the family. Part of me thinks that I should maybe leave it alone. I see some uncertainty in his eyes and don't want to go where he doesn't want me to go. But Jorge feels he owes me an explanation.

"My mom thinks that since we can't afford to give out candy this year, then we really shouldn't be asking for candy from other people." Months later, I would think about this often as I sipped from a coffee cup that took some sacrifice to make.

"What do you think about that?" I ask. And I really do want to know because he's hard to read on this one. What is it that is bothering him? Is it the idea that he told me they didn't have any money, or is it the idea that he can't go out for Halloween? Or, is it something else. He doesn't really pause. He has already done some thinking on his own.

"She's right," he says. "It wouldn't be fair." I look into Jorge's good-natured face and can't help but think of so many other children who might need such a deep lesson in humility and grace. And understanding. See, Jorge doesn't need this lesson. He has more than enough humility, grace, and dignity, for an eight-year-old.

This is hard to sort out for me. Is it because of these lessons that Jorge has the character he has, or is it because of his character that he is able to so calmly absorb these experiences and move on? And would this lesson be sort of wasted on a lesser boy? And what about his mom? How many parents have the kind of character to turn such a tough situation into a positive lesson? I'm just not sure. Jorge seems to have a better grip on it than I do. Of course, I was fortunate enough not to have had that sort of lesson to learn.

There was one thing I was sure about. It was a few weeks later, and I was checking Jorge's homework. I noticed that he was always reading and writing about the same two or three books. And these books were well below his abilities.

"Jorge, what's up with the Winnie-the-Pooh books?"

"These are the only books we have."

"What about the library?"

"My mom works two jobs and it's hard to get to the library."

That night I went down to the mall and picked out the Harry Potter books for Jorge and gave them to him the next day. He thanked me, and I knew how much he meant it. At eight, he was already about as genuine as you can get. And maybe, I thought, Jorge needed a different lesson to learn. Keep smiling and keep hopeful because sometimes good things do happen to good people, the way it's supposed to be. And how could I be wrong about that? After all, I was the best teacher in the world. And I still have the cup to prove it.

Looking Out For Our Own

Flippers. That's how she described them. And she wasn't being mean. Just looking for the right words. I laughed at first. It didn't seem real.

"Come again?" I say.

"Flippers," she repeats. "You just need to see them."

"Where is she?" I ask.

"Take a walk around the room. See if you can find her." It's summer school and my friend has signed on to teach special ed. She's done it for the last three or four summers. She claims she does it for the brownie points. "This should balance out my casino trips for the year." That's what I've heard her say. Couple of things to note here. First, she's not making regular weekly casino trips. And the ones she does make, she talks about freely. Any Vegas trip you can talk about openly is probably not one that requires you to seek out spiritual brownie points. Secondly, even if she were living the "what happens in Vegas, stays in Vegas" creed, volunteering to teach special ed. summer school would still have her coming out ahead.

Summer school is always a mix-bag. Kids are placed as close as they can get it, but choices are limited, so sometimes the best possible placement isn't so great. And, it's only twenty days. By the time you have cracked the code on some of these quirkier, more eccentric kids, it's all over.

You do it because you just have a heart for these kids. A deep reservoir of patience and kindness to tap into. You also do it out of gratitude. Many teachers are parents, too. You do it because you are grateful that these problems are not in your home. You do it because these problems are not in your classroom. It's a way to give back – back to public education by taking on the kids that require you to be fully present at all times, even if only for a month or so. My friend also claims that her summer school money is mad money. It is unbudgeted and hers to do with as she pleases. Rumor has it that the money helps fund her casino trips. It's all a vicious cycle.

Flippers. I wander through the room looking for flippers. Hands, actually. Hands and lower arms that seem filled with loose cartilage rather than bone. Almost rubber-like. I make my way through the room, bobbing and weaving around desks. A bunch of kids recognize me from our home school and smile. I wind up standing right in front of my friend, again having missed her. I shrug.

"See?" she says. "That's how I missed her."

"How did you find out?"

"At lunch."

The school district offers a hot lunch to any kid in town, no questions asked. Since many of the kids who need that free meal are in summer school, lunch is served at the summer school sites during snack time, around 10:30. It's an early lunch, but if you're in need of a meal, time doesn't seem to make much difference.

My friend walks her class down to the cafeteria. She stays with them that first go-around. With a group of young special ed. kids, it's usually best to stick around a while. It's the first day and everything's running a bit slow. In an effort to speed up the line, some of the aides start to bring trays to the kids. A tray is placed in front of Melissa. For a while, she just stares down at her tray.

96

Finally, not sure what to do, she dips her face down into mac and cheese and begins eating. Like a dog with a bowl. My friend takes notice.

"Sweetie, you need to use your fork." Melissa stares, almost afraid to explain herself.

"Do you need some help opening the packet?" The girl nods. My friend takes the fork out of the plastic wrapper and places it on her tray.

"Thank you," Melissa shyly replies. My friend smiles and goes to help another child. Playing with food seems to be big with her group. Tactile learners. One of her kids is busy making himself a small beard from noodles. As far as noodle beards go, it's quite realistic. Not his first noodle beard. He loses some points on realism, as he must keep his head tilted back in order to hold the noodles onto his cheeks. After putting an end to the noodle beard, my friend looks back and notices that Melissa is still eating, face buried deep in the tray. She walks back over.

"Honey, why aren't you using a fork?" It's the sign of a good teacher. You have enough patience to give the child the benefit of the doubt, until there's nowhere left to go. As before, Melissa looks up, almost too afraid to speak. Gently, my friend hands her the fork.

"Here you go." Melissa just stares back and forth between my friend and the outstretched fork, almost panicked.

"I can't," she whispers.

"I'm sorry?"

"I can't."

"You can't use this fork?"

"No."

"Would you like another fork?"

"No. I can't." That's when my friend notices that the child's arms dangle lifelessly by her side. She looks more closely. Her hands seem different. Loose. Disconnected. She sits down and picks up Melissa's hand. It has the feel of thin rubber.

"Would you like me to feed you?"

"Yes, please. But I really need to go to the bathroom first."

"Oh, go ahead. I'll wait."

"I can't."

"Oh. Right." My friend cleans her up and takes her to the

bathroom. The classroom aide spends the rest of the day turning pages for her. They find out that, if you put a pencil between her thumb and pointer finger and hoist her arm up on the table, she can write, using her shoulder and upper-arm strength and range of motion. It's barely visible on the page and a very slow process, but she can certainly focus and get a few lines down for you. And she's happy to do it.

School lets out, and right away my friend calls the special ed. office. Clearly, there's been some glitch somewhere. This is a child who needs her own aide. She needs to be fed, to have pages of a book turned for her. She needs help with her pants in the bathroom. My friend barely gets through the first sentence when a voice on the phone politely stops her.

"Melissa," she says calmly.

"Yes, Melissa. So you know her?"

"Absolutely. It's a rare case." My friend finds out that Melissa's bone disorder is genetic. Her mother has it as well. The long-term good news for Melissa is that when she has stopped growing, an operation can be performed that will give her a fair amount of mobility. Enough to make her pretty self-sufficient.

"So, where is Melissa's one-on-one aide? Surely she qualifies." And here it comes. Listen, now.

"She's not getting one." No other information comes along with this sentence. My friend gives a little wait time, but there's nothing more.

"What?"

"She's not getting one."

"Why not? She qualifies. She can't use the bathroom by herself."

"Yes, she qualifies. But her mother didn't request one. So, I'm afraid she's not getting one this summer."

"Is there a form I can have her mother fill out?"

"No, the summer school deadline has long since passed."

"But this child needs someone to feed her. Someone to take care of toiletries. Place a pencil in her hand."

"I know, but without a parental request, I can't give her an aide, and the deadline has already passed."

Now, let's assume a few things here. Let's assume that Melissa's mother is a negligent parent. Drug dependent. Can't hold a job, hopping from one eviction notice to the next. Filling out paperwork for school isn't even on her radar. Let's just assume it for a moment. She's not. Quite the opposite. But let's just assume she is. For argument's sake. We knew. We knew what she needed. But in the absence of a piece of paperwork, we turned and looked the other way. Aren't we accessories then? We knew she wouldn't be able to unsnap her own pants to use the bathroom. We knew she would have to eat face-first like a dog, unless someone fed her. We knew that someone would need to turn pages for her and put a pencil in her hand. We knew all of that. But, you know how it goes. It's no one's fault. Red tape and paperwork. That's what let her down. Nothing can be done. This tells me two things.

First, this is why you can't run a school like you run a business. If you're the manager of the local burger joint and you have your employees stop offering ketchup and salt packets to people unless they ask, then you save yourself a couple of bucks and help out that bottom line. But if you start cutting services to children because parents don't ask, you may have saved a few bucks, but you've done a tremendous disservice to a child. To somebody's child. To our kids.

But here's the bigger one. This is who we've become. Simply put, we don't take care of our own anymore. Not our own children, our own seniors, our own families, or our own soldiers.

We did at school, though. Turns out Melissa's mother wasn't aware of the paperwork required to get her an aide. She was a kind woman who loved her daughter. And her reply to all of this?

"But I thought they knew about Melissa." She didn't understand. Neither did we. We took care of our own down at school. Aides rotated out of other rooms in shifts. And a child in Melissa's class, a child yearning to be needed and helpful, feeds her at lunch. In our small microcosm, we took care of our own. And I'm sure there are plenty of pockets of folks looking out for their own out there – and in much grander ways than this. But, we do this in spite of ourselves. We do this because our safety net is broken, making us broken. We are only as good as our safety nets. That's who we are. And years of cutting away at our safety nets in an angry effort to weed out small groups of cheats and lazy people has left us broken.

Stripping away at the innocent to find the guilty is no way to run anything. Thing is, most of the time my school district does an excellent job of looking out for kids. But when budgets shrink, you have to start turning over every possible rock. No school, no institution placed in care of our future as a country should have to do so.

Get to the polls. Vote. And when you get inside those voting booths, let's start looking out for each other. Let's start looking out for our own.

Someone To Call

Stranger Danger. They're out there. And they're just waiting for your child to get lost. Maybe, not even lost. Maybe, they just need your child to stray, just stray for a moment from the protection of the pack. Just wander those fifteen extra feet away from the party. Or, maybe, all they need is for your child to turn that corner a little too far ahead of you. And? Gone.

So, as parents, you take every precaution you can. Your child will never turn that corner too far ahead of you. Your child will never stray those few extra feet out of your reach. And, just as soon as you can, you make them memorize their phone number. Now, they need your cell phone as well. Strategically, Mom's cell phone becomes the true priority. Odds are, if you're lost, Mom wasn't home reading while you were out trolling the malls at five.

In my house, when the girls needed to memorize their phone numbers, the numbers were hung in strategic places to help. Since living here, my area code has changed three times – from 213, to 310, to 562. Luckily, I never had to retrain a child during these shakedowns. I think about how many lost kids fell through the cracks during a shift in area code; how many lost children wandered through the enemy territory of the strangers without proper area codes, unable to make the calls that could save their lives. Now, if they got lost during that grace period when the recorded operator told you kindly that the area code you dialed is incorrect, then gave you the new area code, those kids maybe had a chance. But who knows? It can get a little maddening. You always knew the phrase "You against the world" was mostly myth, just something you told yourself to pump up, maybe overcome a current obstacle. But now, "The world against your child" seemed to hold a bit more truth.

When Jordan was five, memorizing her phone number was much harder than it was for my own kids. After a bunch of attempts, she just quit trying. The number was disconnected off and on so many times, what was the point? Which would be more embarrassing at the police department, not knowing your number or calling a disconnected one?

When it wasn't about the disconnected numbers, there was all the moving she, her brother, and her mother did. It was more "squatting" than actual moving. Staying on someone's floor for the week isn't really a move. And, is *that* number your new number? The only calls your mom gets, she avoids. And even if Jordan could consider those numbers her numbers, who would she call when all those strangers out there were more and more part of her world? Lying awake on someone's floor, while the feet of strangers wandered past her head en route to the kitchen or the bathroom. Or the door. Strangers knock on a lot of doors when they should be sleeping.

Soon, there was a number Jordan started to memorize. Her grandmother's. She had to get a message to her, but she couldn't do it in front of Mom. And when they went to Grandma's to borrow money, they never stayed long enough for Jordan to get her chance. Luckily, Grandma still had the old rotary phone she'd had for years. It was the kind that had the number typed in the center of the dial. It took some doing, though. Since she only got a glance at the number every now and then, she had to memorize it in pieces. For a while, all she had were the first three numbers before the dash, and waited for weeks for her next chance to get the last four.

Finally, one night, with all the numbers she needed, while the strangers seemed to be sleeping, Jordan made that call. "Grandma? Come get me. It's really bad." That's all she said. That's all that was necessary. And that's exactly what Grandma did. Sadly, taking the kids from Mom was not as difficult as it should have been. From that point, Jordan had a number she could memorize. More importantly, Jordan had someone she could call.

An Answer To Prayer

I've prayed. Most of my prayers have felt more like desperate pleas. Last-minute bargains I've tried to broker in just under the deadline. To somebody up there, I must seem an awful lot like that relative who phones only when they need money. If I only just prayed more consistently, maybe out of service every now and then, as opposed to desperation, then somehow my prayers might carry a little more weight. I've read that the greatest prayer is a simple prayer of gratitude. Now that's got some real Gandhi to it. There's not a lot of Gandhi to, say, my earnest prayer to keep the washer running long past the warranty's expiration. I just don't see Gandhi praying for the longevity of appliances. Dr. King? Maybe. He was a middle-class working man. I'm sure he stretched a paycheck from time to time.

And I'm sure, people have prayed for me. Let's face it. They've carried me. Most of the time, they've carried me. If it wasn't for my grandmother keeping me in her prayers, I'd be totally adrift. A spiritual nomad, badly bundled by the eye of the storm. And now my own kids throw me in their prayers. Sure, I'm part of that obligatory package. That long list of relatives and friends. I don't mean to brag, but I'm usually third on the list. Each prays first for the other sibling, then Mom, then me. And really, that's about as high as any dad can get. You can't trump a mom or siblings, so coming in right after them is like a first-place finish for a dad. Again, having your kids praying for you has got to build your credibility with somebody up in the front office.

But, the answer to a prayer? Well, for years, I never had that experience. Maybe somebody out there has prayed for me to make a certain decision. But in those scenarios, I'm still just a vehicle. A spiritual tool. Not an end result. And believe me, that's just fine. Seems like an awful lot of pressure to be an end result of somebody's prayer. To be, in essence, the actual prayer. Not a footnote, but the actual prayer itself. The whole reason for getting down on the knee and clasping the hands together. At least, I didn't think I was, until I got this letter.

It's a small note, really. Not quite a full letter. I keep it in my underwear drawer. It's tucked safely behind my emergency stash. You know what I'm talking about. Those ancient few pairs you cling to in the event you run out before the next load of laundry. The note is held securely to the bottom of the drawer by a large, gaudy crucifix. A relative gave it to me years ago and it's just too darn obnoxious to hang anywhere. I'm pretty sure any God with any sense of décor would understand. But to throw it away? I mean, I already don't pray enough as it is, then I go around throwing away crucifixes? Surely that goes on your permanent record somewhere. Even if I threw it in the recycling can, what if it were melted down and made into something awful? What if it were melted down, then sold to some big company with a military contract and my crucifix was used to make weapons of mass destruction? Even weapons of nominal destruction wouldn't help my case. So, as you can see, with perfectly good reason, the crucifix stays in my underwear drawer, beneath my emergency stash, keeping this letter safely in place.

The reason this letter is kept in such an important place is because not only is it the greatest flattery I have ever received, but it reminds me of what's important when it comes to teaching. See, I don't remember the Pythagorean Theorem or geometry proofs because I have a natural inclination towards math. I remember because Mr. Dorner and Mr. Rogers were such great teachers. I didn't start reading Hemingway and Salinger on my own because I just instantly identified with these books. I did it because Mr. Healey and Mr. Lumbard saw me in those books and found a new way to point me out to myself everyday. Truth is, when we think of our fondest school memories, we don't think about geometry or AP English. We recollect the great faith and passion of Mr. Dorner, Mr. Rogers, Mr. Lumbard, and Mr. Healey.

As an elementary school teacher, I don't have the luxury of being so easily identified with a subject. Kids don't remember changing "y" to "ies" with any great fondness or passion. So, I have to make my mark all that much more. Without realizing it, that's what I had been doing with Jack for two years. Two years, I had barely known him. This is how his mother explains it:

Dear Mr. Bowen,

A little story I wanted to share with you. When Jack first started at this school, he started including in his bedtime prayers a plea with God to get Mr. Bowen for a teacher. Every night through first and second grade this was part of his prayers. When he checked the bulletin board to find out which class he was in, his reaction and anger was heartbreaking. A few days after school started, Jack's prayers were answered. When I arrived at school to pick him up, he was so excited when he shared with me that he got to be in your class for math. I was very happy for him. Jack and his friends all look up to you in a very special way. Jack learned a great deal in your class. He was challenged and had great fun.

You can see why I keep this note under the crucifix, behind my emergency stash. Two years. Two years of nightly prayers. All of them barreling along right to me. If you're a teacher and you're doing it right, then you spend most of your day learning. It's not much different from parenting. Kids will teach you who you are and, sometimes, who you can be. A mentor. A philosopher. A much-needed stable factor in a tiny life of turmoil. And who knows, just maybe, if you're working really hard, you can be an answer to prayer.

The Sea

White caps and ocean crests. The sea breeze coats us, then cleans us up. And anybody who walks along a beach looks to be reflecting. Beaches are sacred grounds for dreamers. Dreamers wander the sand at the water's edge, trying to season old dreams or perhaps find new ones. Sometimes you take your losses down there, too.

Beaches hold a mythology for me. They're where quiet dreams go to rest or refuel. It could be the meditative sounds of breaking waves. Or it could just be where God stores these dreams. Who knows? Either way, dreamers like myself wander on long after the sunbathers have gone back indoors.

More and more, when I go to the beach, I'm reminded of a Barry Manilow song. You don't like to let on that an old Manilow tune can move you. It's a sure sign of age and weakness. The song goes on about how he and his father go down to the sea, while their dogs play around in the sand. I used to picture yachting types with sweaters tied around their necks, talking, while purebreds pranced at their feet.

Well, growing up, my father and I weren't those guys. Our dogs weren't those dogs. Strays and mutts, mostly. But we had the sand. The sand and the sea.

My father gave me the sea. It's good to have someone give you the sea. We would drive our old Dodge out to the little beach towns that hid along the Jersey shore. Little roads of cracked gravel. Homemade from before anybody's time. When we hit certain spots, we would turn off the AM radio and listen. Nothing but breaking waves and a chorus of wind chimes. Most of them made from shells. Sometimes we just pulled the car over and listened.

Sometimes we headed for Atlantic City, if we were looking for crowds. We would lean just out over the railings of the boardwalk at twilight. Eyes wide open, staring straight ahead into the last of the sunset.

"Breathe in that salt air," my father would say. And I'd watch him take in deep, heavy gulps as if catching hold of some smell that held his most secret memories. His belly would rise back up over his belt buckle where it originally sat fifteen years earlier. "It'll clean the pollution out of your lungs," he'd yell. I would breathe in and imagine mild soot from off our suburban streets rising up out of me. Teakettle-style. But more than that, the sea-salt cleaned out my thoughts. Mean words still ringing in my head from the playground. Fear. Worry. Just all of it. The pain of being twelve played big baritone notes inside of me. I already had my ghosts. But standing there, listening to my own breath draw deeper and deeper, it was gone. I was made fresh from the sea.

And now I take my own daughter down to the beach, to give her the sea. The dust from the sand fills the cracks in my skin, and my own feet look a hundred years old to me. And when I take off my shirt, I look naked. Skin so pale, it looks like skin you're not supposed to see. I am too much indoors these days. As a child, my skin could keep its outside luster for months. Bits of summer would stay on me sometimes through the first frost. My skin looked alive then, as if it were breathing. Deep breaths straight to the blood stream.

I am now 3,000 miles and twenty-five years away from the Jersey shore, and sometimes I can't help but wonder if a few of my dreams aren't still resting quietly under the boardwalk, waiting for my return. No matter. My daughter and I lean just a little out over the pier, pushing up against gravity. And now it's the pier in California. There aren't too many rickety boardwalks here. The Jersey boardwalk from my childhood was put together with planks that still had bumps and knots rising up out of them. A holdover from some other time.

"Gracie," I say, "breathe in the sea-salt." And my toddler's tiny nose buttons and curls, like it's rolling up its sleeves. She makes a deep breathing noise that even she can't hardly hear. Her tiny tummy expands. Swells almost. Ripe from the fresh sea breeze.

I don't bring to my new little family much in the way of heirlooms. We were more about getting through the day and keeping our chin up. But here, in this one, brief moment, a family heirloom, maybe the only one I've got, gets passed to another generation. And it feels good. It feels good to give someone the sea.

The Tough And The Strong

I didn't want to be this parent. I really didn't. In fact, in the four years my daughter has been in public education, I have done my best not to be this parent: the parent who is also a teacher that winds up down at the school complaining and second-guessing them at every turn. It's easy not to do – when the right sorts of things are going on in the classroom. It's hard not to do when they aren't.

What makes it difficult for me is that for every child that walks into my room, for every activity I plan, and for every way I build relationships with kids, I always ask myself, "Is this what I would want for my own children?" That's the bar for me. Becoming a parent made me a far better teacher. Almost overnight, every child became my child. Our child. And teaching has made me a better parent. More parents than you would want to know about can show you what not to do. And some will show you how to rise above circumstance, above poverty, above disability, and raise the greatest young people you'd ever want to meet. Humble, respectful, grateful, kind, and patient. Parenting can sometimes feel like something you do in a bubble, not knowing if your problems are other people's problems. Teaching can be the same way. In both cases, you close that front door and it's just you and the kids. With about 150 kids in my Title I program, I constantly feel like my parenting abilities are reflected not in just my two girls at home, but also in the stream of little faces that leave our school everyday. So, when I sense that my child is not getting the same from a colleague, it frustrates me.

Of course, frustrated was not how the woman in the office described my tone of voice when I called to make an appointment to see one of my daughter's teachers. Remember being sent to the office? When spitballs were near addictive? Well, that's where I was sent.

When I arrived at school, the teacher informed me, from what could be described as a court-appointed safe distance, that we would be meeting in the office. Aside from instantly feeling twelve, this was also a bit awkward for me because I work in this small district. I'm fairly well known. I do a bunch of teacher trainings and coach teachers each year during our summer school program. So we join the principal as well as my daughter's main teacher.

My daughter actually has four teachers, but I'm only here about one. She goes back and forth between two rooms, and in each room there is a job share situation. It's an arrangement that I'm not too thrilled about. For me, building relationships is everything when it comes to kids. If you don't build those relationships, the best-planned lessons just lay on the page. My daughter loves school and usually talks nonstop about her teachers. But this year, these four are ghosts at our dinner table. It's as if they don't exist. They don't have a community of learners. They have kids and lessons. And there's a big difference. But this isn't why I'm here.

I make the nervous joke about being sent to the principal's office. They oblige me with acceptable nervous laughter. The principal takes out a notepad, takes charge, and begins setting the tone. She explains that she appreciates that I have concerns and she knows I've been in before, insinuating that I've become "that parent." And now, I'm thrown off my game. I wasn't here to talk about that. I was going to let that slide. It was between the teacher and me and it was resolved. But, now that she's brought it up, I feel the need to justify why I had come in earlier this year. I explain that outside of the conference, I had only been to the school one other time. And that was because during the first actual conference, I was shown no evidence of my daughter's progress. Nothing. Not a writing sample. Not a chapter test. Not an assessment of her reading ability or phonics skills. Absolutely nothing. And they knew I was coming. It wasn't an unannounced conference. If they couldn't pull it together for me, what sorts of conferences did other parents get?

The principal stops me. She explains to me that we weren't there to bring up the past. I agreed and wouldn't have done so if they hadn't tried to portray me as the complainer. They want to know why I'm here today. So, I begin by commending the school for taking the lead on our district's Character Counts program. The halls at my daughter's school are named for the pillars of character from the program. My daughter's room is on Respect Road. I commend them for the consistency with which they use the program. Everything the kids do is framed by the pillars of character. Their choices are held up against these pillars. "I like how you showed courage and honesty just now." "Are you showing respect with that choice?" Each character trait is represented by a color and the kids wear a certain color each Friday. A little character-solidarity. And it works. The school deserves its proper credit. They nod and smile at each other.

I also mention how I know that a big component of the district's character push is an anti-bullying campaign. The kids wear pins and wristbands that proclaim they are "bully-free." I then ask the teacher that I have the problem with, "How are you able to teach and model the anti-bully piece, if you're the bully in your classroom?" Nobody's smiling anymore. I've sucked the air right out of the room. Since no one jumps in right away, I continue. "When you yell and use sarcasm as a form of discipline, you humiliate kids in a public forum and you become the bully." By now, everyone has shaken off my initial question and there's a race to be the first one to stop me.

"I do not yell. I use a stern voice," she proclaims with an air of familiarity. We both know she has been down this road before. The principal regains control. "Mrs. Fidler does have a loud voice. And there's no question. She's tough." She hangs on that word "tough" as if it's a badge of honor. She has often referred to herself as tough.

And that's a shame. The goal shouldn't be tough. We should be aiming for strong. Tough sees the world as it is not – black and white. Strong sees the world as it is – infinite hues of gray. Tough lays down the law. Strong emulates the virtue. A supreme example of strong? Dr. King. A supreme example of tough? Bobby Knight. I'd much rather have Dr. King sub in my daughter's class than Bobby Knight.

I go on to explain that, as a teacher, I never appreciated it when parents would assume the worst of me. I turn back to the teacher. "In this case, several other well-respected teachers from your own school as well as parents with honor roll kids here told me that they felt badly that my daughter had to go to your room." Again, the room has lost all air. It's a sure sign that I have hit a nerve. The silence is recognition. And we all know. Once again, the principal takes the reins.

"It's always been my policy never to go on hearsay."

"It's a good policy," I reply. And it is. I don't even bother mentioning that on my list of hearsayers is my wife who, when volunteering, got to watch the teacher in action. She had commented to me that if this was the tone she took with kids when adults were present, what in the world went on when no one was around? I don't bother to mention it because we are all now in a gray area. Really, this meeting was over before it started. It's "she said" vs. "he said." The principal is going to back her staff. It's as it should be, too. I can't blame her. It's how you run a team. You back them as best you can. I would've wanted the same from my own administrator. There won't be any resolution here. But that's okay, I figure. They've been put on notice. So, it's time to wrap things up. I take it from here this time. I apologize for having been so angry on the phone. I make an easy joke about how I'm only five seven and she could've taken me.

The principal asks if it's okay to speak with my daughter on Monday. She wants to put her mind at ease. It's a nice gesture, and I tell her it's appreciated. But, on Monday morning, my daughter has her own plans. This is not going down as just a nice gesture. When the principal wraps up their conversation, restating how the teacher simply uses a stern tone, my daughter won't let that fly.

"No," she says.

"No?" the principal asks. I imagine she's a bit taken aback.

"No," my daughter says again. "My mom uses a stern tone. So did my teacher from last year. This isn't a stern tone. This is yelling." Apparently sucking the air out of a room and leaving little wakes of silence is genetic. The principal thanks her for coming and sends her back to class. I wasn't there, but I know that my daughter didn't come off as very tough that morning. She couldn't have. It's not what she knows. I'm quite certain, though, that her eight-year-old voice cracked a time or two, but somehow let them know that she was, despite a little fear, very strong.

What If God Isn't There?

Conversations can veer away from you. The simplest tangent...gone. Especially with kids. The older guys make a game of it sometimes. Steer you clear off topic, hoping you won't find your way back to math or Spanish missions. And they truly bait you. They pretend to be interested in your life, insisting they love that story about the subway guy who claimed to be a Martian. And all of a sudden, you're no longer in your classroom. You're at a cocktail party and all the important guests just can't seem to get enough of you. And then the bell rings and you realize you've been shamefully duped by a couple of ten-year-olds, who wooed you into believing they cared. Used up, is what it feels like. How could you have lost twenty minutes to ten-year-olds? It's something that scares me about getting older in this profession. When the elastic of the mind starts to weather, the kids will be able to run smaller and quicker circles around me. Snapping back to topic won't be easy.

Man, they just play you. They know your weaknesses. High-school memories. Stories about your own kids.

Funny thing is, though, they really do care. Just watch them sit up straighter and clean it up for you when the principal walks into the room. They've got your back. You're one of them. You've been taken under thirty little wings and you couldn't ask for more.

Sometimes, the conversation can veer in directions you never intended to go, and getting out can be a delicate matter. See, they're not old enough for your opinion on anything with any weight to it. Lighter stuff, you can sidestep.

"Is Santa real?"

"He's real to those who believe." See that? Sidestep. Political style. No definitive answer. But actual politics? God? Social issues of the day? On any of these, your opinion is not just your opinion. It's gospel. You're a teacher. And not just any teacher. You are their teacher. The answer man, dolling out knowledge in digestible chunks. You're the guy that knows three ways to do long division. Their parents, mere mortals on a good day, know only one. You have earned their trust and respect, almost blindly, to the point where they long for your high five in line.

"Pick me! Pick me!" they plead, their dirty little palms pushing forward, like little extended bellies, hoping it's the hand you pick. They flap in the air with no impulse control. And you want to tell them that getting a high five from a middle-aged white guy isn't all they've made it out to be. But you can't. You need their belief fully suspended to keep the show afloat.

Usually, when that heavier topic pushes itself up to the forefront, there are a few easy stock answers to pull from.

"Mr. Bowen, who did you vote for?" Who did I vote for? The current administration is ruining the country. My country. They're trampling civil liberties and passing on billions of dollars in debt to you and your kids. See, that's the answer that bubbles to my forefront. But the answer they get?

"Voting is a personal matter. That's why it's done in a booth with a curtain." Issues of sex, anything even remotely sexual, are always something you should "discuss with your parents." And awkwardly, sexual bad words are easily squelched the same way.

"Do you know what that means, Alex?"

"No."

"Ask your mom tonight."

"No way!"

"Oh. So you do know it's an inappropriate term to be using here at school."

"Yeah."

There's also a small gray area in this whole matter. Definition vs. judgment.

"What's an atheist, Mr. Bowen?" See, I can answer that one. Definition. Not judgment.

"An atheist, Jill, is a person who believes in no God."

"You mean, like they just don't go to church?" The notion of complete disbelief is hard to take. I begin to get a little nervous. A follow-up question is always worrisome. But, still, this is just clarification. That's all. Just a little clarification.

"No, Jill. It's more than just not going to church. It's a belief that when we die, we don't meet God. We just die. Death is the end." I get a little more nervous. I just used God in more than one sentence. This is public education, and I can feel a legal team somewhere whispering in my ear, "Get out now." I take another look at the textbook and start to hunker down. I hadn't noticed it the first time around. My bad. It wasn't the focus of my lesson at all, but now, taking a closer look, it was about to be.

The pie chart broke up modern day San Diego into religious beliefs. What percent were Baptists. What percent were Mormons. And, yes, what percent were atheists. And now that we know that atheists don't believe in God, this pie chart has sparked a lot of interest. And just whose grand idea was it to sneak this pie chart into my public school textbook? Why don't they just sprinkle traces of cocaine all across my lesson plan book and plant whiskey in my art supply cart? Initially, we were going to compare and contrast our small California town, from a hundred years ago to the town we all shared today. I even had pictures spanning decades of the area's history. Shopkeepers with handlebar mustaches stood on dirt roads between horses, sweeping the dust away from storefronts carved out of knotted wood. But that lesson was going to have to wait for tomorrow.

"What's a Mormon?" Now, I'm not that up on Mormons. I know

121

fragments of the John Smith story, but not enough. Apparently, it's okay, though. Somebody else does.

"Mormons are those crazy guys on the bicycles."

"Are they those crazy guys on the bikes, Mr. Bowen?"

"Yes," I say, instantly realizing I just accused the Mormons of being crazy.

"Really? You think they're crazy too, huh?"

"No, I just meant that they are the guys on the bikes, that's all."

"So, like God just told them to go around, riding bikes?" A kid cups his hands and does his best God impersonation.

"Mormons. This is God. Go ride your bikes." It's a good improvised God and a pretty funny line. Before the laughter dies, we're off again.

"And, what's this Baptist thing?"

"I'm a Baptist," Allen says proudly.

"So, Mr. Bowen, does that mean that Allen is going to hell?"

"I'm not going to hell!" Allen yells, a bit annoyed by eternal damnation.

"No. Allen is not going to hell," I say, assuring Allen, yet knowing that my authority doesn't extend quite that far.

"But he's not a Christian. He's this Baptist thing."

"The Baptist religion is part of Christianity," I say.

"But just a part," she counters, using my own words against me. "So, Allen could still go to hell, like, maybe, for a little while."

"I'm not going to hell!"

"Allen doesn't have to go to hell," suggests Laurie. She smiles. "We could pray for him. Let's form a prayer circle around him." A prayer circle in fifth-grade Social Studies. Maybe I was going to hell with Allen and all the rest of the Baptists. Kids actually start to move. I see the glint of a circle start to form around Allen. I squelch this one immediately.

"Remember our class rules. No one gets up without permission."

"Not even for a prayer circle?"

"Not even for a prayer circle," I say with a stern voice. I drop a few octaves to make the point. It's time to return to Social Studies. It's time to return to a topic that won't require me to seek union representation at a formal hearing.

"So, who's right?"

"I don't know." I can answer that one. No judgment. Just a bit of honesty. But no one likes to hear their fifth-grade teacher claim that he just doesn't know. It tells them that this is a big one. And with that, the room gets very quiet. Much like a moment of silence. And then Jill, who started this whole business, asks, "What if atheists are right, Mr. Bowen?"

Again, "I don't know."

"What if God isn't there? What if we all get to heaven and God's not there?" I have to laugh.

"Jill, do you realize what you're saying?"

"Yes," she says in earnest. "What if we all get to heaven and the atheists are right and God is not there?" I pause. Everyone thinks on Jill's words. They sit and hover. Jill looks to me for an answer. I am, after all, her teacher. I am her answer man. But it's really Jill who's holding the answer of the day. God? Well, she couldn't be so certain about that anymore. But herself? She would be there. For sure, she would be there. In herself, she had unconditional faith. And maybe that was the best kind you could possibly have.

The Warm-Fuzzy Lady

She had a kit. The warm-fuzzy lady actually had a kit. As near as we could guess, it was filled with warm-fuzzy supplies. She brought it with her every Thursday afternoon. Some of the fifth grade though, speculated that at the bottom of the bag she kept a shot gun for the day when her over-the-top, gleeful persona became too much, even for her. I remember a day when she had just finished clapping the most annoying happy clap that made me deeply embarrassed to be in her presence, and then, abruptly, went rummaging through the bag. The boy next to me leaned across the aisle.

"Today's the day," he said knowingly. "Make sure you stay down and keep your head covered," he added.

Actually, the kit was filled mostly with read aloud books. Sometimes during a story, her voice would travel three to four octaves over the course of a single sentence. It was a lot like listening to someone sing the national anthem, wondering if they've got enough steam built up to hit the rockets red glare. And once, she pulled a purple feather boa from the kit, to explain the concept of the warm-fuzzy. That's how her nickname was born. A genius move, really. She gave herself her own nickname. Just ridiculous enough to stick, but not so ridiculous that she couldn't go out in public. We were, after all, New Jersey ten year olds. We did have the capacity to make adults cry.

And the warm-fuzzy lady never had just a regular face. It was either a game-show-host smile. Broad and plastered. Too many buffed teeth drying in her mouth. Or, if she had to read or discuss a sad or unfortunate moment, then she was deeply sad. She managed to make her whole body sad. Drooping, heavy shoulders. You could actually see how osteoporosis would look on the warm-fuzzy lady in thirty years. Her lip would swell too, and the weight of it would drag her face into her dangling love beads.

In the kit, she also kept a squishy ball with an angry face printed on it. We were supposed to squeeze it when we were angry. The problem was that she only had the sample squishy head. It seemed like a logistical nightmare to have to call the warm-fuzzy lady and have her meet you so you could borrow her sample squishy.

She also taught us how to do the silent scream when dealing with our anger. The silent scream is pretty self explanatory. Wide open mouth. Clenched fists. Tense neck and shoulders. Our little bodies shaking, quivering slightly. It was presented as a better way to deal with our anger. Sadly, it didn't take into account how ridiculous it looked. The peer pressure from people ridiculing you would only double your anger, escalating the chances of some real violence. To be fair, the warm-fuzzy lady did tell us many times to find a quiet place to do the silent scream. But, we were thirty-six kids crammed in one room for up to six hours. And our playground? We had lines nine to ten deep at the slide. Four to five deep just on the one nicknamed the baby slide. Sometimes, she had us practice as a class. It was after lunch. No one felt very angry. We had been lulled into light comas from a starch fortified lunch of tater-tots, some sort of casserole, and gravy. But after doing a few silent screams, we started feeling pretty amped. Riot incited, almost. After the third silent scream, boys started staring each other down. Eyes and chins suggesting, "Yeah...come on!" An occasional girl started to cry, coming to some catharsis after the fourth or fifth silent scream.

What I was most agitated about when it came to the warm-fuzzy lady was the concept in general. It was the seventies and the warm-fuzzy movement was in full swing. The goal behind her weekly visits was to get kids in touch with their emotions. As a ten year old boy, this really didn't interest me. See, the people in my family who were labeled emotional were a little bit nuts. A great-grandmother who could cry on a dime. An aunt who would scream over the mundane. I wanted no part in this. As near as I could tell, at ten, I had only two emotions; good and not-so-good. There just didn't seem to be a rational reason to go looking for more of these emotions.

All of this made me pity Jack Winslow. He was a boy in our class and, yes, the son of the warm-fuzzy lady. I made a mental note to myself that if I was ever invited to Jack's for dinner, I wouldn't go. I couldn't imagine sitting through a whole meal with her. What nightmare was dinner at the Winslow house? Were there a minimum number of emotions each person had to share during the meal? If you had an angry moment during the day, did you have to grind your fist into your mashed potatoes until you owned the emotion and allowed it to pass through you? Could no dessert be served until tears were shed? No way. I was never having dinner at the Winslow table.

Here's the day I most remember with the warm-fuzzy lady. It was a typical Thursday afternoon and she posed a question that was supposed to guide us into the icky world of emotions.

"What are the things we most need in life?" her voice skipping octaves along the way. It was a no-brainer. Food, clothing, shelter. There's water, of course, but I was sort of lumping water into the food category. Finally, I thought, a question I could wrap my head around. Immediately, my hand went up. The warm-fuzzy lady made positive eye contact with every person who put up their hand. Validation was in abundance.

"Yes, Maria?" she said and managed to raise three octaves in a question that only had two words.

"Love," Maria said, more asking than telling. The warm-fuzzy lady tried to broaden her smile, but quickly realized that it was impossible, so she nodded her head instead.

"Excellent answer, Maria." Was she kidding? Sure, a little love

127

was nice, but who was going to love a starving, naked, homeless guy? The warm-fuzzy lady wrote the answer on the board. I didn't take it seriously. She was, after all, the warm-fuzzy lady. She had to validate all answers. Even ridiculous answers like Maria's. I kept my hand held high.

"Donald?"

"Hugs?"

"Excellent!" She actually clapped. She clapped for hugs. She stopped clapping just long enough to get the answer on the board. Now, I understood the idea of validating answers, but come on. Clapping for hugs? Without your food, clothing and shelter, you're going to be too weak to hug back and too delirious from starvation to even realize you're being hugged. Everything just sort of spiraled down from there. Grandparents. Smiles. Pets. And the warm-fuzzy lady listed pets on the board. Now the term pets covers a lot of ground. This included, I supposed, pets that were not mammals. Now, critical to survival, according to the warm-fuzzy lady, were those little gold fish you win at carnivals and sea monkeys. Once gold fish and sea monkeys made the list I put my hand down. It was like listening to a foreign language that I couldn't decode. I had enough of the warm-fuzzy lady.

So, did the country, I think. When the eighties rolled around, warm-fuzzy ladies across the country were laid-off. Once education shifted from creating good citizens to good capitalists, warm-fuzzy ladies were sort of counter productive. That one afternoon a week could no longer be spared.

I had forgotten all about the warm-fuzzy lady for years. For decades, really. But, over my time in the classroom, she sort of started to creep back up on me. Years of children punching each other with little or no escalation. Straight to violence. Kids from angry homes. Kids bounced from home to home. Kids riddled with abuse. Like a long lost saint, I have called upon her in times of need.

"You ever hear of the silent scream?" I hear myself say from time to time. Of course they haven't. And I remember the part about doing it alone. I suggest a bathroom stall these days. Here's the thing. Without knowing it, I have become the warm-fuzzy lady. I have a few less octaves in my range and I've done away with the feather boa. But it's true. Slowly, I have evolved into a new breed of warm-fuzzy lady. The ten year old boy I once was would surely squeeze the squishy head to death if he ever found this one out.

Hugs. And love. They've become pretty important. Sure, they're never going to surpass food, clothing, and shelter, but they are climbing. Sea monkeys are not.

Where have all the warm-fuzzy ladies gone? They're shuffling through bookstores. Listening to public radio. Just trying to weather the years of anger and "me first." To be honest, I wish I could find mine. I'd thank her. Who knows? Maybe we could have dinner and just sit around discussing our feelings. I have a few more of them these days.

Hitting The Mark

He makes small talk with me for a while, then finally comes out and says what's on his mind.

"So, you think that kid's got a shot at hitting the button tonight?" He's got a sports-moment tone to his voice. I nod.

"He's got a real shot at it." He returns my nod. "He hit it three times this afternoon," I add. The father looks impressed, almost soothed, by this new information.

Something occurs to me. The kids have really talked this performance up at home. Attendance is high for this one. Families sit together, a few generations deep. Sure, families are here to see their children sing and recite. And beam. But, they are here too, for something more. Every parent and grandparent sitting in our cafeteria that night knows all about David and the button. Everyone wants to see him hit the mark.

David is a special needs student up against some severe physical and cognitive challenges. And tonight, he plays an important role in our spring performance. He must hit a button at just the right moment in the show and a recording of some of the kids will come up. David can be found most days in his classroom. He sits, speechless, face twitching, head doing a constant bob. The attention, the timing, and the motor skills it will require to hit this button taps into as much skill as David can possibly call on. There was debate amongst the staff about even having David do this. You never want to set a child up for failure. Never set a child up for failure in front of a classroom. And in front of a crowded assembly? But, now and then, you've got to lean on a little magic. Some risk is required. Hope for more from a child and just maybe they'll pull it off.

In rehearsal, David's hit-and-miss. You can tell many of the kids are worried for him. Teachers too. We set up a "B" plan. A student agrees to walk over and hit the button for David should he lose concentration or hand control and miss the moment. But you can tell she hopes she doesn't have to do it. Nobody does. We are all deeply invested now.

It's the single most important moment of the show. And not because the button keeps it all rolling at a pivotal spot. We're doing a lot more here. We're validating a life. We're validating hard work and effort for a child who, decades ago, would've been dismissed. When you think about strides in education, David is one of them. Remember, every child is entitled to a public education. It's why private schools send us back every student who isn't achieving at a suitable rate. It's part of their pick-and-choose luxury. It's not so here. And special ed. isn't the dumping ground politicians like to make it out to be. These students don't easily fall through the cracks. The law won't allow it. Every kid has goals, and all goals are measured and reassessed. Hitting the button meets a fine motor skill goal for David. Participating in the spring program with dozens of regular ed. students meets our school's commitment to mainstreaming special education students at every opportunity that presents itself.

Our school has several special needs classrooms, and some mornings I look out on that playground and watch children in wheelchairs turning jump ropes for others. And I see there, the country I want to live in. On that playground, I see a small slice of the next generation one-upping us in tolerance. In dignity. In respect. As you would hope. As it should be.

The sound of the lift hoisting his chair up onto the stage echoes through our cafeteria. There is silence as the machine moans. The button is placed on a tray attached to his chair.

On the other side of the curtain, I notice that David is wearing a suit. And a tie. I think about the extra effort it must have taken to get his constricted, balled-up arms into the jacket. Or how time consuming it must have been to get a tie around his constantly fidgeting neck and bobbing head. But, it's showtime. We all must look our best.

The lights dim. Parents shuffle to their seats. Little girls smooth the pleats in their skirts one final time. Little boys make sure they're standing where they need to be. The curtains rise. The music begins.

On cue, kids sing and parents clap. But every song feels like an opening act. We are all waiting for the moment. We all know why we are here. A young girl holds a pure note and lets it linger out past the music. It should be her time to shine, but I can see her begin to glance at David. The spotlight shifts over to the young boy, horribly hunched over. His jacket is a mangled mess. There is a pause and nobody seems to be breathing. And, with perfect timing, he hits the mark.

The house comes down. Without hesitating, without even thinking about it, parents stand. It's a thunderous applause. Touchdown. Grand slam. It's a very simple moment. But, no question, it's the best moment of the school year. The most important, too. David smiles. His ever-moving head rocks back and forth.

His hitting that button is a gift. No smaller than any talent displayed that night. And, we are all better for knowing him. Our ovation is our thank-you. His broken laughter is his thank-you in return. I wouldn't trade it for the best reading or math lesson of the year. Standing and clapping, we seem to remember what's best in ourselves. We have met every need. We have raised the bar now for every child to be his or her best. This is what it really means to leave no child behind.

As I write this, summer is coming to a close. My daughters have been very quiet in the kitchen for too long and I have lingered here at the computer. A new school year is about to start. If you work with children, here's hoping you find every child's gift and every child's need. And, this year, may we all hit the mark.

A Place To End

Two reasons to end here. The first? I couldn't afford the therapy. See, my daughter, Grace, makes a few major appearances on these pages. Starring roles. And Clare, her little sister, is only referred to once, buried in a story about Grace. Just an extra on the set. It was never intended to be a slight. See, Clare was born while most of these stories were written. Just born too late. Really. But to have your father publish a book that includes your sister and not you? Therapy. Hours of the stuff. And I can't risk just balancing it out with a story or two in the next one. If there is no second book? Therapy. We're right back to therapy.

The second reason is bigger. Fuller. A bit more genuine. It's this. You should really meet Clare. My wife, Grace, and myself often joke that one day Clare will up and leave us. We just bring her down. She's simply a better person than the three of us. Eventually, she'll seek higher ground. It ain't us.

As I've said before, usually I learn more than I teach when I'm with kids. And it's not so much learning. It's more remembering. All of us, at one time, had the hope, the honesty, the integrity of a child. But, we compromise. Bargain so much of it away. In the end, all of it for chump-change, really. We nickel and dime ourselves. The worlds we create become so small. They can't possibly hold an idea as grand as hope. Or faith. Or kindness. Sometimes, if we're lucky, we can stretch these little worlds of ours just enough to let kids in. Even one can do it. These little seeds. And, they will hold our hope and faith and even our warmest smiles for us. All for safekeeping. Just waiting for us to remember. But, I fear, the longer it takes us to start to remember this sort of stuff, the sooner they begin to forget. It is not easy holding someone's faith for them, if they don't seem eager to find it.

Just this year, Clare helped me remember something that I put right back into my teaching. It was something I remembered instantly. Before Clare gave it back to me, it was just information rolling around inside me. It wasn't latched onto anything. No reference point to get back to it. And sometimes, it's all in the timing. Sometimes we remember something just before we need it to lean on. I like when it works this way.

So, I'm packing Clare's lunch for school. It's first grade now, so getting to take a lunch is a very big deal. Clare likes to inspect my work. She's watching me, building up to a question. I can tell. On her face, I can see her internal hemming and hawing.

"Daddy?"

"Yes?"

"Can you pack me an extra one of those little cakes?"

"I don't think so. That's a lot of sugar for a little girl."

"The extra one, I'm going to give to Alex." My mind searches a bit. Where have I heard that name before? And then it hits me.

"Clare, isn't Alex that kid who picks on you?" Clare nods, and right away I'm thinking extortion. "Isn't he that kid who threw the sand in your eyes that time?" Clare nods. And, after this second nod, my blood starts to heat up just a bit. The Jersey boy I used to be starts rising to the surface. "Alex. The guy that pulled your hair the other day." Again Clare nods, seemingly oblivious to the sound case I'm building against Alex. Yeah right, like this kid is really getting a cupcake out of me. Clare is actually getting annoyed with me.

"Yes. It's all him. There's only one Alex in my class."

"Then why are we giving this Alex a cupcake? He's a mean dude." Clare thinks for a moment. I can tell she has a clear answer, just not clear words right away. I watch her go through a brief rehearsal in her head.

"I know he's mean, but maybe no one showed him how to be nice. If he doesn't know, then maybe I could show him how it feels to be nice." And there she is. My small holder of hope, getting me to remember important stuff, and stretching my tiny world a bit. Sure enough, a week later, I'm using Clare's lesson.

A kid in my reading class is just about failing everything. It is the fallout from the services we provide. Diego has tested out of our English Language Learner program. That's the good news. The bad news is he's out there now without his support system, just flailing around. Totally overwhelmed. The counselor asks if I can just keep an eye on him. So, we arrange time after school to get caught up, but when you're failing everything, time is a valuable commodity. So I decide to talk with his P.E. coach. Maybe he can miss a little P.E. and he can work with me to help him get caught up. As I explain the situation, I can tell the coach is annoyed with me. I'm the Pollyanna. Do-gooder. Protecting slackers at every turn.

"Why this kid?" he finally asks.

"Why not?" I answer. This annoys him even further.

"Well, we've got all kinds of kids failing. Why does he get special treatment?"

"It's help. Since when did basic help become special treatment?"

"But you can't help them all. That's why this is special treatment."

"No, I can't help them all. And I'm not supposed to. I'm just supposed to help the ones that fall into my lap. If everybody helped the kids that just fell into their laps, then the treatment wouldn't be so special. It'd be commonplace. As it should be." He pauses. Little does he know, I had just been schooled on all of this by Clare, only days earlier. I'm on top of my game. "If you don't believe me, ask Clare."

"Who?" he asks, a little confused.

"Clare. She's a consultant for the district." He nods, not sure what to say. But, it's just like Clare's bully. The schoolyard has plenty of bullies. Alex was just the one to fall into her lap. Diego?

Right into my lap. Clare falls into my lap all the time. She loves it there. But really, little does she know that most of the time, it's the other way around. I'm an adult with a poor memory for the bigger ideas out there. It's all right, though. I've fallen right into Clare's lap. And it's a good place to be.

In Closing

I've heard it said that we are often asked to teach the lessons that we need most to learn. I've always taught kids to dream big. And, as I finish this first book, I have finally allowed those hundreds of kids that have graced my classrooms over the years to teach me the lesson I was called on to learn. And I thank them all.

Printed in the United States
131942LV00002BA/7-15/P

9 781432 724535